FREE WILL, DO YOU HAVE IT?

Behaviour is the Result of Process,
Rather than Choice

Tellwell Talent
www.tellwell.ca

ISBN
978-0-2288-3713-8 (Hardcover)
978-0-2288-3711-4 (Paperback)
978-0-2288-3712-1 (eBook)
978-0-2288-5486-9 (Audiobook)

DEDICATION

I have dedicated this book to several people who have been an inspiration to me and had a significant impact on my life. My mother, Catrien Westen (1921-1985), with whom I had countless deep conversations and whose wisdom and understanding have contributed to a foundation of sincerity, peace and direction I will treasure for the rest of my life. My father, Jan Kral (1920-1976), for his giving nature and readiness to help others when they needed his service. My mother-in-law, Lucille Mayes (1925-2017), who became like a second mother to me and whose acceptance, love, compassion for others and quiet wisdom remain a daily guide for me.

Unfortunately, I make this last-minute entry of dedication in loving memory of our daughter Marielle van Duin-Kral, who unexpectedly passed away November 10, 2017, at the young age of 40.

Recognition of those whose contribution and encouragement were significant and greatly appreciated

I am forever grateful for the hard and dedicated work of Lil Loewen for her invaluable assistance and tireless encouragement to help put this book together. She helped me define my thoughts for efficiency and clarity and was always an encouraging inspiration to me in her corrections, advice, and constructive criticism.

I must extend my appreciation to my great friends Robert Loewen and Ron Wiens, who over the years listened patiently to my numerous test runs of my concept, waiting for an argument that would strengthen my thoughts or amend them in order to fill the holes. They gave valuable feedback, often resulting in the words: "Yes, but . . ." That was what I admired in them as it forced me to discover thoughts in my concept that could reasonably and logically answer the "buts."

Our daughter Catriena Kral inspired me with her countless contributing arguments and continuous interest in the development of my concept. At the end, she wanted to know what conclusion I discovered, and I told her she had to read the book to find out.

I'd like to thank Tellwell for their great assistance with editing while enabling me to still write my way.

I must also thank the many people I passed, had brief conversations with, listened to, and observed. They also provided inspiration without realizing it and as such contributed also.

Last but not least I am grateful to my wife, Bernice. Her contribution was invaluable as she listened to my many expressions of unfinished thoughts. Her questions always led me to dig a little deeper to finish my thought processes. She always remained a source of inspiration and encouragement. Without her inspiration, constructive criticism and support, this book would not have been written.

TABLE OF CONTENTS

FREE WILL: DO YOU HAVE IT?
INTRODUCTION

This book goes far beyond the issue surrounding free will. Indirectly, it relates to all the human behaviour of any society. It expands our awareness and shines a new light on each one of us. The greatest danger humans face is the power of bad influences. It is all around us, and it is in us. This power of influence is greatly underestimated and that makes it even more dangerous. I am not saying that all influences are bad, but the greatest danger lies in the power of bad influences. There is no anti-influence pill like there is anti-virus software to protect us. Awareness offers us the best possible protection whereas ignorance leaves us vulnerable, unprotected, and unaware of our ignorance. To see the whole picture, this book should be read in its entirety.

"Why?" is likely the most asked question in the world. When people make choices and we ask *why*, it strongly suggests that we believe there must be a reason for the choice made. It also suggests that we do not easily believe that the choice was simply made because the person wanted to make that specific choice without any reason at all. When we ask another person *why*, it opens a controversy because we believe we can make any choice we want. Most of us believe we have free will to do so. We should simply accept that the other person made the choice because they wanted it. That should be the end of the conversation; however, it seldom is. Why do we need a reason? Can't we just accept that people make choices for no reason at all? After all, is that not the essence of free will?

Free will does not require an explanation nor a reason, it means that the choices we make are free from any influences and are made without any reason. Yet we have a difficult time accepting that something is done for no reason at all. We persistently want to know why, and don't settle for just any answer. This fact suggests that we do not believe that we make a choice because we simply want to, but because there is a reason to make the choice. No choice is made without a reason, influence or other stimuli, whether it is known or unknown to us, whether it takes place at the conscious or subconscious level. Many may stop for a moment and ponder this thought, but others might dwell on it for a long time. I make this statement because the thought is novel, revolutionary, daring, and challenging to the conventional thinker.

The fact that you are reading this is because you chose to pick up this book. Perhaps you even bought it. You probably had a reason for the decision you made. Whatever your reason, and whether you are aware of it or not, the fact is there was one. You may consider it revolutionary and find that, when applied, it shines a completely different light on society and people we encounter. Perhaps you find it enhances our understanding of human behaviour in a new way. However, it may take some time to adjust to this novel approach because you may not have seen or read it before. After reading the book, the alternative to what is discussed may seem questionable, and yet it has been our belief forever that we have free will. If there are flaws in this belief, as I see it, I have tried to expose them throughout this book.

The content is written in plain language and is generally easy to follow. The degree of difficulty does not lie in the content of the book but rather in the radical approach.

Behaviour is something we manifest continually. There is a fundamental relationship between behaviour, the brain and the *I*.

> "I, the one who is me, am a vehicle for the manifestation— through behaviour—of the outcomes of brain processes that have reached the threshold of manifestation, where the awareness factor of each outcome immediately, through a new process, impacts that outcome at the moment I become aware of it, resulting in instant changes (outcomes) as they appear and are manifested through my behaviour while it provides me with the human feeling that I, the one who is me, am making the choices I want and do as I want, being unaware of any brain processes that take place and produce outcomes I manifest in my behaviour."

We make thousands of choices daily. Our bodies function without our conscious and decisive participation, as none of us decide to keep the heart pumping or the stomach digesting our food. I have never heard anyone say, "Oh, I almost forgot to keep my heart beating," or, "I forgot to have my stomach digest my food for the last few days." That sounds ridiculous because we all know that our body functions by itself. When we drive a car on the highway we function continuously, which includes the many small adjustments we make steering the car, looking in the mirrors, adjusting the speed of the car, applying the brakes, looking at the road signs, changing radio stations, having a conversation with a passenger and so on. Many of those behaviours just happen. Most do not need our conscious participation. Perhaps we don't look at them as choices but when we steer the car a little to the right, we could have done it to the left as well, couldn't we? If that is true, you could say the choice was that we steered the car to the right. How often have we said, "If I had known that, I would not have done it." We hear it all the time when people say, "I did not have a choice." I believe that most people have at one time or another asked someone, "Why did you do that?"

When we follow a murder trial and hear the commentaries, we know that the word "motive" is often brought up as an important factor. It suggests that we want to understand why a murder was committed because it seems that we believe that there must be a reason, *a motive* for the action. Voters who can elect the next US president are often exposed to masterpieces of manipulation because the candidate's goal is to get their vote. An election is all about votes. Thus, each candidate tries to give voters a reason to vote for them and therefore need to influence or manipulate those reasons. Most of us have been in a situation where we tried to convince a person to do (or not to do) something. We give those people reasons—at least what we believe to be reasons—to act or not to act in a certain manner. The question whether our actions are simply a matter of choice remains.

In all of this, our brain stands at the centre and cannot be left out of any discussion about our behaviour and the decisions we make. The brain is our central command post, and nothing gets done without its involvement.

I hope that the reader finds the following ideas on free will presented in a fresh and exciting way that challenges their conventional beliefs.

CHAPTER 1

HOW ONE QUESTION STARTED IT ALL

More than thirty years ago, a friend suggested we should visit someone he knew very well and who enjoyed philosophical talks. He said that I would enjoy talking with him. We drove to his home where he lived with his mother. We were introduced and before realizing it we were engaged in a lively conversation. Time passed without being noticed. When I realized what time it was, I said, "Sorry, but I have to leave." Under normal circumstances a few "thank you" comments are made and then you are on your way. No one thinks any further about it and life goes on. This time was different. Right after I said I had to leave, someone asked whether I knew why. *Of course I know that*, I thought, *Otherwise I would not have said that I had to leave*. So I responded, "Yeah, I have to buy some groceries and finish some work at home."

The other person's remark has had a profound impact on my thinking. For over thirty years, I have thought about it so much that I have built a concept around the answer. He said, "You have to leave because there is nothing else you can do. Do you believe that you have free will?" *Ah*, I thought, *that is too easy and I am not falling for this*. So I replied, "OK, I will not leave but stay." Looking back, I realize now that my reaction was one of ignorance as I had helped prove a point that I will use often in my concept. At the time,

I had no idea about its value and usefulness. You may be thinking, *No way, this is absurd. Of course you could have done something other than leave if you had wanted to. How could he ask you whether you believe you have free will? Of course, we all have free will.* If true, it should be easy to defend.

After I left, that question would not leave me alone. Every time I decided to do something, it would pop up. I began asking myself whether I did have free will. I almost felt embarrassed because it was not imaginable that I couldn't choose whatever I wanted. For days on end I asked myself, *Why do I do what I do? Why do I make the choices I make?* My brain went to work and produced numerous reasons for my choices. Some choices were so obvious that it would be absurd to even contemplate having made a different one. Gradually I started to focus on the reasons behind my choices and I began to ask myself what it would take to make a different one. I imagined that it would require coming up with different reasons because the reasons I had could not be used to support a different choice. *If two plus two supports an outcome of four, it cannot also support an outcome of five,* I thought. This made a lot of sense to me at the time. It had not occurred to me earlier to look at my choices in a numerical manner. Numbers are simple to use and understand. They make logical sense. At the same time, I thought it could not be that simple. I knew that although numbers are logical and easy to understand, mathematical equations can be very complex. Even so, it was a start to look at choices and reasons in terms of numbers. Later it proved to be even more helpful.

Choices and Reasons

Let us continue by looking at a link between choices and reasons. If you have tried to convince someone to do something, did you give that person all kinds of reasons that, in your opinion, would influence them to make the choice you wanted them to make? If you were not successful have you ever said, "I don't understand you, why wouldn't you do it? I have given you all the reasons why it is the best choice and you still won't do it." This strongly suggests we believe there are reasons that support those choices, perhaps they may even determine them. On the other hand, it also suggests that the same reasons that cause one person to make this choice do not necessarily cause another person to make the same one. If we try to convince another person to make the choice, we most often bring up the factors we believe would accomplish that, because in most instances we would make that choice for those reasons.

During a presidential election campaign in the US many candidates know which issues are most important to the people they are speaking to. The candidate will present solutions to those issues that they anticipate most people will like. If immigration issues are extremely important in one region and unemployment a bigger issue in another, the candidate talks about these issues where they exist and provides solutions the audience wants to hear. Sometimes gun control is an issue in one region, where they want stricter gun control laws, but in another region, they do not. However, if the candidate is in favour of gun control, they will try to avoid talking about that issue where people do not want this. They will focus on other issues where possible solutions to other concerns are established. The whole presentation is to inspire, and I would add, manipulate the people so that they will give them their vote. Every election campaign is designed to accomplish just that: get the votes. Give the voters *reasons* to vote for them. However, it is important to keep in mind that no two people have the same brain structure nor do both brains work the same. This will come up later, when it will be discussed in more detail.

People are Different

Going back to the point where we try to find reasons that influence some people to make a particular choice but not others, we could ask why anyone thinks that what influences them should influence others. On the surface this may sound reasonable but when we dig a little deeper we recognize that we are not all the same, but more likely, we are very different from one another.

To point out some of our differences we can look at our upbringing, personal experiences, goals, beliefs, education, cultural background, preferences and so on. Now we need to go back to that inspiring question of whether I thought I had free will, to which I responded, "Of course, simply because I can do what I want."

I started to abandon that belief as I gradually became aware of new information. I began saying: "It all depends." It depended on which choices I had to make, whether my mood was a factor, whether I was sick or not, whether I had the money, and so on. It was clear that this simple statement had big implications. If our choices depended on factors that were obvious, where was the line? Which factors would have a bearing on our decisions and which would not? Were there factors we were not aware of but that would still affect our choices? One child is afraid of the dark and another is not. It appears that the child who is afraid of the dark was often scared by others playing tricks and having fun with the lights out. We can all agree that the child is not thinking about those experiences when in the dark, or telling herself that she has to be afraid because someone previously scared her. That this child is fearful of the dark is a conditioned response; it comes upon her when the light disappears. I began to recognize the power of influences as well as individual brain structures that process information and contribute to each person's uniqueness. As the first influence is being processed by the brain, it contributes either noticeably or not, yet influences the development of perception.

None of us can take a tool and consciously change the structure so that information will be processed as consciously desired. At that moment I realized that yes we can, perhaps not consciously as with willpower, but in another form. I thought about the effect of drugs and alcohol on the brain and how they alter the way it processes information and stimuli. Medication is often used to improve or eliminate certain behaviours.

Sorting Through New Thoughts

I had arrived at a point where I needed to sort through my new thoughts and organize them logically, although they took me outside the box of conventional beliefs. I became convinced that we are exposed all the time to a stream of information. Much of this information affects our brain, as stimuli, without us being aware of it. The structure of our brain is different from that of any other person's, and our genes play a significant role in that. When the embryo begins developing in the mother's womb, the brain develops as instructed by our genes. We could say that development follows a set of instructions provided by the genes. Only from this perspective could I begin to make sense of our decision-making process, and I was convinced that my thoughts, inspired by that first question, would lead to an outcome independent of any assumptions. The essence of that outcome was waiting to be discovered.

In time, I started to reorganize my thoughts. Perhaps that would bring new perspectives. I had learned during this process that reorganization of thoughts would expose elements that remained hidden if the light hadn't shone upon them. The most important discovery of this realization would come towards the completion of my concept, when the process presented a discovery, but we have not arrived at that point yet.

A summary of the steps of several thoughts in building a seamless new model follows below. It could explain how our behaviour is formed, with some choices made and others not. I found that this was a process that would make discoveries leading to the outcome just as only the main path in a maze would lead to the exit. The point I am trying to make is that I am not steering this process; I just want to understand and know. That happens only when all the cards are on the table, no matter how absurd they may seem. If they are absurd, the process will eliminate them as long as I prematurely do not. Until the moment they are naturally eliminated they may serve a purpose: to find the outcome. Our brain-processing structure varies from person to person, and this explains how the same stimulus may not produce the same outcome. I pondered this thought for a long time and started to think about more complex factors that affect our decision-making processes. I believe now that the brain-processing structure could be affected by stimuli. The stimulus or influence is not only processed to produce an outcome, but affects the brain process itself. This is a major factor in Procirclism: what is processed not only produces an outcome but it simultaneously affects future processes. Therefore, if it were possible that the same stimuli could be processed one after another, the outcomes would not be the same because the first process would also impact the brain, and as such, affect the next process, producing a different outcome.

What I mean is this: any number (information is represented by a number in this example) we receive will be multiplied by 4. When we receive the number 3 (the number that represents the information we receive), the outcome will be 12 (3×4). When we receive the number 7, the outcome will be 28 (7×4). Each process does not only produce an outcome but also has a direct impact on the next process. In this example, where the information number (3 and then 7) was multiplied by 4, it changes to the next process of information to be divided by 4. Instead of multiplying it by 4 (in this example), the given number may cause the process to change to a division by 4, or a multiplication by 5 etc. This means that not every process affects the next process in the same manner. This illustration is a simple way to show that any stimulus or influence is being processed and produces an outcome while at the same time it affects the way the next stimuli is processed. The brain is a dynamic organ.

I must clarify that each number represents a certain stimulus and when I mention a number as an outcome, it represents certain behaviour. Each stimulus and behaviour is unique in its smallest detail, because individual perception plays a role. When more than one person reacts to witnessing a car accident, each person has their own reaction to this. They may be similar, but when we look deeper at the reactions and examine the details, we recognize the difference between the reactions, therefore each individual will see differences. It is my belief that today we may not be able to recognize all the details of such perceptions yet. Witnessing a car accident as a stimulus causes certain emotions triggered by our perception of the accident.

When expressed in time it may look like the following. There is a car accident. When we talk about the accident, we also speak about time. The accident itself may occur in one or two seconds from the moment of impact until the moment the accident ends. From the first millisecond to the last, a stream of stimuli is sent to our brain. Our brain receives these stimuli but depending on the brain structure it may not be able to receive all of them. Countless tiny pieces of information of the accident are sent as stimuli to the brain. Each tiny piece of information (stimulus) is received by the brain as the perception of the individual. In other words, the brain perceives it in a certain manner and without our conscious participation. The speed is much too fast for us to be aware of. It does not feel this way, and we cannot know this from experience, we can only deduce it. How we perceive a stimulus depends on the brain function at the moment of impact. Every experience from our past contributes to this perception. We have millions of pieces of information (stimuli) received and processed by our brain while at the same time and at lightning speed those stimuli also impact the brain process itself. That means that the next stimulus would not have produced the same (to its smallest detail) outcome if the brain had not previously received and processed stimuli.

New Ideas Often Meet Resistance

Before I continue to the next chapter, I must tell you that my new ideas have not been met with enthusiasm and agreement. Although I discussed the topic with a select group of people, I did not receive a consensus, but the arguments against my ideas were an inspiration. They brought me back to the drawing board, but not once did they make me wonder whether I was going in the wrong direction.

I would even sit in restaurants and ask the waiters whether they believed we had free will. Reactions to this question were precious and they demonstrated that hardly anyone had given it any thought. Facial expressions screamed concern for my sanity. I must admit it was fun.

I recall a time when I was in the hospital recovering from minor surgery and the nurse came along to check whether the other patients in the room and I were awake. As she approached the patient beside me, I said, "Nurse, nurse, do you think we have free will?" She responded but not in the way I had expected. She said, "I will check with you a little later when you have fully woken up." As time went on, I built up consistent and logical arguments for my ideas and a few people began to say that I made some good points. I started to receive questions and challenges rather than the dismissal of my ideas, yet nobody fully agreed with me about free will. In my arguments, I suggested that we do not have free will. Free will means that any choice we make is completely free from any influence. The ramifications of saying we do not have free will are tremendous. Most people don't doubt we can make any choice we want; you may share that opinion. Yet digging a little deeper, we have found our brains do not process similar information in the same manner and do not produce the same outcomes.

In mathematical terms, we could say that one brain represents the number 8 and another brain represents the number 10. Now let us assume that the influences on both persons (one with brain 8 and the other with brain 10) are represented by the number 4 (same influence, same representative number). In this example, one person will arrive at an outcome of 32 (8 × 4) and the other person arrives at an outcome of 40 (10 × 4). The numbers 32 and 40 represent outcomes of brain processes (8 × 4 for one brain and 10 × 4 for the other brain). For one person, 4 (influence) is processed by 8 (brain), and for the other person it means 4 (influence) is processed by 10 (brain).

To simplify the brain process I have used multiplication. It is much more complicated and not yet fully understood. Accepting this makes it easier to understand that the same direct influences (influences immediately preceding an action, sometimes called *triggers*) will not always cause us to make the same choices.

Why does it cause one person to make a choice and another a different one, after being exposed to the same direct influences? In the next chapter, we will explore this issue further.

Could you imagine your best friend, who has never left her country, suddenly calling you from the other side of the world? It would go something like this: "Hi John, guess where I am? I am in Russia, I just arrived an hour ago." It is not likely that you would say, "Great choice, have fun and see you when you're back." Even if you said this, I am sure you would be asking yourself what in the world she's doing in Russia. It is more likely you would ask her directly what she was doing there. It is clear that we cannot find a reason or direct influence for our friend suddenly traveling to Russia but that she just did it because she wanted to. "Impossible," we'd say. "There must be a reason. What influenced her to go to Russia?" If our friend gave us a reason, such as looking up a person she met two years ago while vacationing in Europe and who gave her his address at that time, some of us would say, "But that is no reason to suddenly get up and go to Russia." It demonstrates that what causes one person to do one thing does not cause another person to do the same. This suggests that something more, something all-inclusive that demonstrates a difference, must contribute to the choices we make. Something much less noticeable, perhaps not even observable in the common way or not yet known, must be a factor in the choice. Why? Because 2 + 2 cannot be 4 as well as 5.

Two Plus Two is Four

A robber plans to rob a bank. Two obvious questions about possible influences behind this action come to mind. First, we could ask ourselves why she wants to commit a robbery in the first place. The second question could be why she wants to rob a bank. A multitude of reasons lie behind someone wanting to commit a robbery. As everybody knows, banks are all about money. Along this line of thinking we may believe the robber assumes that there is money in the bank so we could establish a possible reason why a bank is targeted.

We may have a little more difficulty finding a reason for why the person wants to commit a robbery in the first place. I don't believe that any person is convinced that the robber woke up one morning and just decided to rob a bank for no reason at all. One would likely say, "If she has no reason, why is she doing it?" Whatever influences the robber would not necessarily cause other people to commit a robbery. The influence could be that the robber has fallen on hard times after losing her job. Many other people have experienced the same thing but not all began to commit robberies.

Another factor might play a role in this scenario. We could assume that the robber is aware that she could go to prison if caught. Yet that did not seem to deter her from robbing the bank. Many of us would question why someone would risk their freedom to commit a crime. Some may think, *If I risked my freedom, I would have to commit a robbery that made it worth the risk.*

In another scenario, you are driving at 90 km/h but the speed limit is 80 km/h. You know that speeding might result in a fine, but you continue at the same pace. Why? One reason could be that you have experience that on this stretch of highway the police do not enforce the speed limit until the speed is 95 km/h. However, the next day you drive 99 km/h on the same stretch of highway. The reason for speeding might be that you need to be somewhere at a certain time. Suddenly, cars from the opposite direction flash their headlights—a common signal that there are police ahead. You slow down. Why? Is it because of the police, the fear of getting a speeding ticket, both, or something completely different?

Then there is the person who does not slow down even when warned the police are ahead. Is it possible that this information causes you to slow down but it does not cause the other person to? If everything is equal then it is unthinkable that we have two different outcomes. In mathematical terms, it would mean that 2 + 2 = 4 but also 5. Therefore, the all-inclusive reasons for each of their actions must be different. Assuming that signaling police are ahead is a fact both experienced and represented as the second number 2 in our mathematical expression, then the first number 2 cannot be 2 for both people because the ultimate outcome is that one person slows down (where the equation equals 4) and the other person does not (where the equation equals 5). The first number 2 must therefore be different in one of the two people. Actually, it does not matter what this number represents in this example. If it represents the brain, and the brain of one person is represented by the number 2, then the brain of the other person must be represented by a different number because we know that the outcome is different for them both (slowing down and not slowing down). My point is that something must be different. The brain, stimuli or previous brain-process outcomes must be different—no matter how minuscule—to produce different outcomes (manifested behaviours).

The all-inclusive reason is that all factors contributing to the choice we make because of the complex brain process answer why a choice is made. Based on the example of the two drivers, there must be contributing factors to the different results. The observable fact shows that both drivers were speeding and both received warnings that police were ahead. Therefore, any other contributing factors must be different—no matter how slight—in order to produce two different outcomes: slowing down and not slowing down. There is no other possibility, otherwise each driver's action could be represented by the mathematical factor: $2 + 2 = 4$, and that is not the case, as one slowed down and the other did not.

Pondering the Same Question

These are the kind of thoughts that entered my mind as I continued to ponder the question: Do you believe you have free will? I realized that there was a full range of contributing (if not determining) factors for all our actions. As such, any specific behaviour goes beyond the understanding that our behaviour is based on free will, not influenced by anything. When we take an umbrella with us, it suggests that we want protection against rain or sun. When we buy a snow blower, it suggests we expect snow. If a person living in the Dominican Republic purchased a snow blower, many of us would ask why.

As mentioned before, I continue to ponder this question and believe that when we keep asking it, something magical happens. I speak from my own experience when I say that our brain goes to work without our awareness, which is fascinating. Thoughts pop up in our mind, seemingly from nowhere. In my case, these thoughts relate to the question I have been trying to find an answer for: Do I have free will? Sounds easy, doesn't it? Some of you may say it is either yes or no. This is true. I could choose either. Then I would ask myself why I chose yes, for example. Now, our approach to the question influences the outcome. If my answer is yes, I would look for proof that we have free will. If I answered no, I would look for evidence to prove we don't have free will; I wanted to find the answer via the question and not from a predefined belief; I wanted the answer to flow from the ponderings of the question; I wanted the answer to appear from the bottom up, and that required an open mind; I needed the question to take the lead; I had to consider everything, otherwise I would imprison myself in the box that existed and was already defined.

This is where I believe the unconscious played a vital role as my brain went to work. I may not be able to explain the process, but I am aware of my experiences. I experienced with amazement that certain thoughts, unprovoked, would suddenly pop up in my mind. I began to recognize the development of my concept when I watched the news, spoke with people, listened to people, and observed people's actions, including my own. In simple terms, I could say that all actions have a purpose and there are a host of contributing factors. When paying attention to this phenomenon, I started to recognize that different actions or behaviours arise from different contributing factors. As time went on, I felt that my concept grew stronger and became self-adjusting; it tweaked itself as part of its developing process.

CHAPTER 2

THE POWER OF INFLUENCE AND INFORMATION, CALLED STIMULI

The development of our brain begins in the embryo, with DNA regulating it. At one point in its development, the brain receives stimuli that could be sound, temperature, movement and much more, that affect its development. In this case, we understand stimuli as anything that affects the brain but whose instructions are not encoded in DNA. Thus, up to a certain point in its development it can be said that the brain is pure as it is not yet affected by stimuli. After that first stimulus, the environment has begun its work as an influential factor in the development of the brain and thus in our behaviour. Any environmental stimulus to the brain can never be undone.

When we take a glass of clear water and drop red dye into the water, we see that the color of the water changes. That color will always remain part of the fluid in the glass. From that moment on, any other color we add is mixed with the first drop of red dye and produces a different color. The strength and volume of the dye contributes to the new color that is created. We take another glass and also fill it with clear and pure water and then let a tiny drop of blue dye fall into it. We notice that the colour in this glass is different from the colour in the first glass. Now we let a drop of yellow dye fall into each glass and we see that the colours in each glass remain different because they were already different from each other. The effect of the first colour of dye remains an influential factor in any new colour that will appear after mixing another colour of dye into the the glass. Any new colour added affects the fluid in the glass, and when mixed it produces an outcome as a new colour appears. In fact, the colour of the dye that will be added at any given time will never show in the glass in its full essence. So, a green dye added to an existing mixture of colours will not cause the fluid to become the same green. When we add a tiny bit of dye with an extremely weak colour to a mixture we may not see a change in the colour of the fluid in the glass afterwards but that does not mean there is no change. If that tiny bit of colour we add does not change the colour of the fluid in the glass at all, then a lot of that same colour does not change the colour of the fluid in the glass either. In other words, if we have nothing and multiply it by ten, we still have nothing. The color of the fluid in the glass is changed after any dye is added, even if we can barely see it.

We make new discoveries all the time. At one time, people thought that the earth was flat; now we know it is round. There has not been historical evidence of people having fallen off the edge of the earth nor of captains of a ship who had to make a sharp turn to avoid drifting off the edge of water into space. In the past, people were declared dead when they were still alive, but we could not recognize the subtle signs of life. So, what is not noticeable does not necessarily mean it does not exist.

Everything we experience on either a conscious or unconscious level is considered a stimulus to the brain. Every stimulus must reach a threshold for the brain to be able to process it. This process affects the brain and the outcome. That means that the previous process and the outcome of that process affect the next process. When a home has been robbed several times, the people who live there may get frightened. Any sound in the house may cause fear. It is an understandable response. After they have installed a security system, they may no longer be frightened, and now feel secure. Yet, when they suddenly hear a loud noise in their backyard, fear may creep into their mind again. This fear disappears when they realize the sound is caused by a strong wind that blows the branch of a tree against the shed. The experience from people who have never been robbed may be totally different under similar circumstances. This shows how a stimulus (robbery) produces an outcome (fear) and that outcome affects the next process of a stimulus (hearing a sound) which causes another outcome (some fear). No outcome was the result of choice. Hearing a sound caused by heavy wind may not produce an outcome of fear related to a possible robbery. In fact, it is much more complicated and is why our behaviour differs so much from person to person and moment to moment. For example, if a teenager takes a stone and scratches along the side of a brand-new car while the owner approaches his car, the car owner may want to get the teenager and so runs after him. Then, when a group of teenagers suddenly appear and run towards the car owner, he may stop running after the teenager. If a person suddenly appeared with a gun and pointed it at the car owner, he might not even have started running after the teenager. To understand what the brain processes as stimuli we must divide what looks to be single events (such as a car accident, a hockey player scoring a goal, a tree falling or a child sliding on the ice) into the smallest increments the brain can process. The increment that is being processed cannot be divided any more for brain processing purposes. It is the smallest increment that the brain can and does process as stimuli.

Brain Processes

When I try to illustrate some integral parts of the concept of Procirclism, which I will discuss in more detail in Chapter 3, I resort to numbers. Earlier, I assigned numbers to a single brain process of a stimulus and assigned another number to the stimulus.

Each brain process is unique to everyone. Our genes and individual experiences, internally or externally stimulated, contribute to this uniqueness. When talking about our genes we must also pay attention to the latest developments in science.

Scientists are working on being able to alter some genes that can affect the color of our eyes and how tall we may become. It is anticipated that eventually they may be able to alter individual genes to the point that the person with altered genes may be smarter, taller and stronger. The person may have a brain that functions differently and may be free of certain diseases and likely much more. This implies that the behaviour of such individuals is also altered. When altered genes affect how our brain processes stimuli, it indirectly affects the behaviour of that person. There is no will involved in this process. Although not necessarily recognized for this purpose, it supports the arguments I make in favour of my procirclistic model. The uniqueness of each brain means, for example, once a number has been assigned to the brain process of one person, the same number cannot be assigned to the brain process of another person because that person's brain is different. In addition, what is being processed (stimuli) is not the same for each person due to the complexity of the stimuli. Several people may witness the same event but each person perceives it differently. Thus, for example, if we assign numbers to stimuli, the numbers will have to be long because they are unique for each stimulus. For instance, if 278.39576621095 is assigned to one stimulus, and 278.39576621096 can be allocated to a different one. Because the difference is so minuscule, it may not be noticeable. We have *what* is being processed, called the stimulus, and we have *how* it is being processed, called the brain process. For instance, there is a clear distinction between the brain processes of someone with autism and someone without autism. If we assign a number to the brain process of someone with autism, that figure will be noticeably different from a number assigned to that of someone without autism. When the brain of someone with autism processes a stimulus (represented by a number) and produces an outcome, that same stimulus will produce a different outcome for someone without autism, resulting in a different behaviour.

The Perception of Stimuli

A stimulus is perceived by the brain and that means it is subject to individualized perception. Perception causes us to interpret or experience the same event in ways that are different from person to person. Each brain perceives a stimulus in its own way. For instance, we may think that when we witness the same event as another person, we also perceive it in the same way. In other words, all stimuli of this event are represented by the same numbers for each individual brain, thus we incorrectly but automatically assume that witnessing the same event means its stimuli are also perceived the same. It suggests that an event, processed by the brain as a multitude of stimuli, can be perceived the same, in its fullest details, by different brains. That is not possible because we all perceive things differently. In general, it may seem we perceive things the same way, but when we start looking at the details, we start noticing differences in our perceptions. The closer we look at the smallest details, the more we start noticing the differences in our individual perceptions. When we divide any event into the smallest possible parts (increments/stimulus) that our brain can process, we notice differences, depending on our ability to observe them at that time. Not being able to observe them does not necessarily mean they do not exist. As we make progress in discoveries, we are constantly able to see or recognize things we previously did not. That happens in neuroscience.

When two people look at a red rose, we assume that we all see it in the same way. Let's assign a number to the red rose. It is 23.457, based on the assumption that everyone sees the rose the same way. If they do not see it the same way, then the number representing it is different for each person. To demonstrate that we do not all perceive something in the same way, I use the following example. When a person who is colorblind looks at a red rose, they perceive it differently because this person cannot see the color red in the way the other person sees it. Thus, the number assigned to the stimulus (red rose) is different for both people. It cannot be 23.457 for both people because they did not perceive it in the same way although they both looked at the same rose. Therefore, what seems to be one and the same thing (stimulus) becomes different as people perceive it uniquely.

We have seen that events are a multitude of stimuli. Everything that is being processed by our brain I refer to as stimuli. It is important to have a closer look at events and how they relate to a stimulus. To do this, we must talk about details, increments, and how they relate to stimuli.

A Car Accident

We usually talk about events as single occurrences. If, for instance, we witness a car accident, we talk about what we saw. One may ask, "Did you see it happen?" and when we respond yes, we will likely begin to talk about it. To us it seems one event, just a car accident. However, if the accident were to be filmed and replayed in slow motion, we would clearly see that a car accident consists of a multitude of small fragments.

In theory, we could divide the event into smaller fragments from 1 second to $1/10^{th}$ of a second, to the point of infinity. If we could show the film in increments of 1 second, we would see a series of snapshots representing every second. When we talk about the car accident, we talk about a single event that comprises the accident from start to finish. When we describe it in more detail we are talking about the smaller increments, the smallest of which we are unable to detect with the naked eye. We usually recall more rudimental details in larger increments than seconds. We may recall that one car suddenly applied the brakes because a child ran across the road and the car behind it followed too closely and was unable to stop in time. It slammed into the back of the car ahead, bounced off it and became airborne, flipping over and landing upside down on the road. Replaying the film of the accident in slow motion we see the details more clearly. At this slow pace, each picture looks almost the same as the previous one, but it is not an exact duplicate, as that would mean that during playback of the film we would see just one static picture and no movement or change.

Our brain processes the whole event in increments. Thus, the process of a multitude of stimuli represents the whole event. This implies that only the smallest possible increments are processed. Together the increments make the whole motion picture of the car accident. Each increment must reach a certain threshold for the brain to be able to process it.

If it were possible for the brain to process the car accident as one single stimulus, we could, for example, assign the number 11 to this stimulus. For this to be possible the brain would have to decide what constitutes one event and then process it as one stimulus. The brain would have to decide when an event starts and when it ends. How would it decide what an event is? Would it be the car accident with the people running towards the accident and helping any injured persons? Would the first car hitting the second car be one event and processed as one stimulus? It is impossible to imagine which concept could regulate how a timely event, which consists of a multitude of stimuli, could be selected from that multitude of stimuli and then be processed as one stimulus. In that case, a timely event selected and processed as one stimulus by the brain would represent one static picture as opposed to a motion picture. Each shot is a stimulus, but multiple shots cannot be one stimulus.

Yet, as the event takes place, that one shot (stimulus) cannot represent the time it took for the event to take place. How can we take a single shot of time that represents five minutes? If we can take only one shot that represents an event lasting five minutes, it must be done as follows. We take 5 times 60 pictures. These picture frames must overlay each other, thus representing five minutes of action, which is the event the brain must process as one stimulus. In this case, we use the negatives of the pictures because they are transparent. We lay the 300 negatives of pictures on top of each other (300 pictures taken at one second intervals represent five minutes; the time of the event to be processed as one single stimulus). Now we take one picture of that pile of negatives and call that one picture the one stimulus representing the event that took five minutes. What we see is one big mess and because of this, the picture of the 300 overlaying negatives will not show anything clearly.

There is another reason why the brain cannot process an event, representing a period as one stimulus. If it were possible to process an event that started at 5:30 p.m. and stopped at 5:40 p.m. as one stimulus, then we would not be able to recall or experience an event that started at 5:35 p.m. and stopped at 5:43 p.m. It could not be assembled because there would be no data available in the brain for this demand. For example, when relating it to a motion picture, we would have one convoluted picture representing the time from 5:30 p.m. to 5:40 p.m. because we only have one picture of an overlay of 300 pictures. There would be nothing that represents the period from 5:35 p.m. to 5:43 p.m. because it would be hidden in the single shot (of the overlay of 300 pictures) of the period from 5:30 p.m. to 5:40 p.m. There is no *one* shot of the timeframe from 5:35 p.m. till 5:43 p.m. nor are there single shots of the smallest possible increments during that period from 5:30 p.m. to 5:40 p.m. (remember this period was processed in one stimulus). Thus, the timeframe between 5:35 p.m. and 5:43 p.m. cannot be assembled because that time frame is not represented in its smallest increments. As a result, the brain is not able to recall that timeframe. That is why the brain only processes events in the smallest possible increments it can process.

The brain cannot recognize events representing a larger period than the smallest increment it can process. It cannot recognize stimuli the way we become aware of it after the stimuli have been processed and pushed to our awareness screen. I use the expression "awareness screen" for an illustrative purpose. We can look at it as a computer screen. We must imagine that we can only see what appears on the computer screen. In similar fashion we can only be consciously aware of something after our brain has pushed it to our awareness screen. There are certain thresholds. For instance, we cannot experience the smallest increments in single fashion. We experience these increments seamlessly and fluently (even when they appear as flashbacks). Continuous processes of the smallest increments the brain can process take place when they reach the brain as stimuli and have reached the threshold necessary for stimuli to be processed. When we witness a car accident our general response is the outcome of all brain processes of each increment of the accident. Our response is not the sum, nor the average of all single brain processes of each increment of the accident because of the complexity of each brain process. Different parts of the brain may be involved and include stimulation of emotion as well as the application of possible conditions regulating each brain process. There is an interaction and correlation between each stimulus (fragment of the accident) that is being processed and between the processes themselves. Each outcome of a brain process not only produces another outcome but also affects the quality of the next brain process of a stimulus. There are no averages in this concept, nor sums. Our response or reaction is noticeable, as it is manifested through our behaviour. The process of the stimuli is seamless and our general response is seamless as well, meaning that we are not fragmented in our general response to the accident. Other people see it as our general behavioural response that includes associated feelings, and not as a fragmented, piece-by-piece reaction. A single number does not represent that car accident, to which I referred earlier with the number 11. It is made up of a multitude of smaller increments. One increment is always the smallest possible stimulus our brain can process. Here is an example:

> Let us say that the following numbers represent the smaller increments: 2, 1, 2.5, 4, and 1.5. That is 11 in total, which is the number we assigned, as an example, to the car accident. We have seen that the brain cannot process events that are not divided into the smallest possible increments; such is the case in the example of the car accident; it may be perceived as one event or thought of as one stimulus, but in essence it consists of a multitude of the smallest increments of the accident. The brain only processes the smallest possible increment. Any multitude of stimuli can produce an event that represents a period that cannot be processed as a single stimulus. Thus, for processing purposes of all stimuli, the number 11, representing the car accident from beginning to end, is not and cannot be recognized as such by the brain. For the brain, the number 11 that I used earlier in my illustration does not exist. It can only be assembled from a multitude of processed stimuli representing that specific period.

A Motion Picture

A motion picture is made up of small sections (fragments) and after being edited (processed), the sections produce the full seamless motion picture. We call it a movie. We can talk about a movie as an event. As we previously read, for processing purposes our brains cannot recognize an event such as a toddler running cross the lawn as one stimulus. It is impossible to shoot a movie in one frame. A video camera takes a multitude of shots in rapid fashion that result in a motion picture or movie when it is played back at a certain speed. We don't see the single shots, but we see a movie.

Cartoons are made up of many drawings that are shown in rapid succession and provide the illusion that the people and objects are moving. It is not perceived as an illusion because we see them moving. Our brain, when it produces outcomes, does something similar when it processes stimuli and we become aware of it as it unfolds in the form of seamless motion pictures. When we talk about it, we relate to them as events such as a soccer game, a family dinner, a Christmas party, a vacation, etc. We do not see fragmented picture frames but one continuous motion picture. Our reaction or response includes an emotional experience. We are not consciously aware that our emotional reaction reflects the outcome of brain processes of a multitude of stimuli (increments).

Events Consist of a Multitude of Stimuli

Our brain cannot present the outcome of the processes of all stimuli to our awareness because our awareness could not keep up with it. As the stimuli are processed and produce outcomes, they feed our awareness. Our awareness is subject to a protocol that regulates how outcomes of processed stimuli are displayed in the arena of our awareness. We know from our own experiences that we are not aware of fragmented outcomes, but smooth and seamless outcomes, as in a movie. Our brain processes a multitude of stimuli, which are the smallest increments the brain can process. The process of stimuli during a timeframe produces events as we understand them, talk about them and experience them. Such an event can be, as we read earlier, a car accident. For our brain, the event as a single stimulus does not exist. For the brain, the event as we describe it when we talk about a vacation, storm, movie, birthday party etc. does not exist. When we look at a large painting, we do not think that the painting could not exist were it not for the small details that make up the finished painting. Paintings begin with painting a small segment. The orderly assembly of smaller details represents the finished painting. Our brain is not interested in a total product. It does not know what a finished product is. The brain is mainly occupied with processing each stimulus and producing an outcome. Somewhere else in the brain, when outcomes are pushed to our awareness, they are assembled according to a protocol so that we experience (become aware of) a painting or can recall a vacation as a memory from beginning to end.

Each Brain Process Affects the Next One

All stimuli (increments) are processed at lightning speed and produce outcomes that affect the next process. Each brain process also stimulates emotion. As such, emotion affects the outcome of the brain process and subsequently affects behaviour. It also affects how the next stimulus will be processed. If we are exposed to an explosion and the sound damages our hearing so that we are deaf, then we experience nothing but deafness after that. When we look at each stimulus that is processed, we will come to one stimulus that is processed and its outcome is without sound. The process and the outcome of the previous stimulus affects the new process and results in an outcome that is now without sound. So here it is quite clear that a stimulus affects our hearing, and after losing our hearing any following stimulus is processed and its outcome is without sound. Another example would be if we were walking and suddenly somebody hit us. This would produce an outcome as we reacted to it. It may be in the form of anger, hitting back, fear, or something else. We may still be affected by this experience for quite some time without being consciously aware of it. It may become evident during future walks in how we experience certain events. However, the aftereffect may also be less obvious but nevertheless present.

Threshold

Only when a stimulus reaches a certain threshold is it observable and can be processed by the brain. A threshold is a condition that must be present for something to be processed by the brain as a stimulus. For instance, we are not able to hear all the sounds that are around us. For us to hear sounds they must be within the threshold (frequency range in this case) for us humans, before we can hear anything. The threshold for something to be observable is related to our ability to observe something that is within that threshold. If that threshold is related to the brain process, it means that the brain cannot process a stimulus that is below the threshold of the brain process, whatever it may be. This threshold for something to be processed as a stimulus is extremely complex and dynamic, meaning it can change under different conditions.

The quality or functionality of the brain plays a big part in the threshold and when we think about brain damage we can understand this. Thus, a stimulus must meet certain criteria for the brain to be able to process it. The threshold is part of the regulation that is encoded in the brain and may have come from its DNA. It regulates the brain process.

The conditions that regulate the brain process, such as a threshold, can be static or dynamic. A static threshold remains always the same where a dynamic threshold can change, depending on various conditions. How they change follows a protocol encoded in the brain. This simply means that it is not random. Actually, nothing that happens in the brain is random. There could be several conditions regulating the brain process and interacting with each other in a complex manner. Thus, as we cannot hear all the sounds that exist, so each brain does not process everything unless it is within the threshold. My brain for instance, at this moment, cannot process an event that is happening right now on the other side of the world as a stimulus, because I am not aware of it.

Brain Processes Produce Outcomes We Manifest as Behaviour

We are all affected by stimuli that reach our brain, mostly through our senses, and are processed by the brain. What I call a stimulus or stimuli can be described as our experiences, whether consciously or sub-consciously. These stimuli can have a devastating effect on our brain. Post-traumatic stress disorder (PTSD) is an example of this. People suffering from PTSD may experience extreme difficulties not of their own fault. It is the effect of the outcome when the brain processes stimuli that causes great stress. It is well known that PTSD affects the behaviour of those experiencing it. With PTSD, the brain processes stimuli differently than it does when there is no PTSD. It can also cause stimuli to be perceived differently. When the brain processes a stimulus and produces an outcome, it affects the following processes of stimuli. In the case of PTSD, it is most often observable through the manifestation of certain behaviour. Does that mean that all people who are exposed to the same conditions experience the same outcomes? No, not necessarily. As mentioned before, each brain is unique. In addition, all past experiences affect the brain process, contribute to the way new stimuli are being processed, and influence the outcome and thus behaviour. In this case, the greater outcome is PTSD.

Emotions

Any stimulus may activate our emotions. In other words, whenever the brain processes stimuli, according to the individual's brain's coding and instructions it also regulates the emotional involvement in that process. Subsequently, it is part of the outcome produced by the process. Therefore, what we experience as single occurrences such as the screaming of a child, the scoring of a goal during a soccer match, a tree blowing over in a storm, a village being destroyed by a tornado etc., is in fact not a single occurrence; it is a seamless stream of smaller events or stimuli, each processed by our brain at lightning speed, which we become aware of as moments. These moments depend on our awareness platform to handle them and keep up with the speed in which the brain presents the processing outcomes to our awareness. In my expression of "awareness platform," the word platform relates to the ability of our awareness (or if you like, *awareness screen,* and you can imagine it as a monitor) to handle what the brain processes and we can become aware of. We can think of it as a monitor that displays information, movies etc. However, sometimes a monitor may not be able to show certain information because it cannot handle it and the screen remains blank. Only when our awareness platform can handle it can we become aware of it. The brain keeps processing and producing outcomes regardless.

Our feelings are a result of the outcomes of brain processes and have an impact on the process itself. Not all outcomes producing feelings reach the threshold of our conscious awareness, but they can still affect our behaviour without us being aware of them. Feelings are part of our life. In every moment, we have feelings, but we are not always aware of them. Most often we feel as we do without being consciously aware of the kind, type or intensity of the emotion. Who has never been asked whether you are in a bad mood? For those of us who have been asked, we may not have realized that we were in a bad mood or that it was so obvious. Perhaps we denied it while knowing we were in a bad mood. Anxiety is another emotion that is apparent in our behaviour and is not difficult for others to spot. Again, we may not even realize we are anxious. In previous examples, it showed in our behaviour, especially to those who know us well. Happy emotions are just as easy to see. Emotions are stimuli that are part of the brain process that produces outcomes manifested through our behaviour.

How often do we stop and focus on our feelings of the moment? In other words, how often does a stimulus produce an outcome that draws attention to our feelings at that moment because the outcome is pushed to our awareness. In plain language we might say, "I'm trying to focus on my feelings," or, "I need a moment to get in touch with my feelings." When stimuli activate our emotions and are manifested, the result is expressed in our behaviour but is not always recognized as such. Do we consciously determine what and how we feel? No. Feelings are the result of a complex brain process that includes all past processes. Not all our feelings are related to present stimuli because past stimuli have influenced our emotions in such a way that they affect how present stimuli are processed. We generally state that our past experiences have affected us in such a way that they influence how we experience something today. Thus, the complex brain processes go as far back as the moment the first stimulus affected our brain and was processed. In every process all of our past is included regardless of its significance according to social, cultural or moral standards, for example. Because of this all-inclusive process, we can say that behaviour is always perfect (perfection meaning that something is as it is and cannot be different, unless something else is different). This definition of perfection is concrete and not subject to interpretation. It is as simple as 2 + 2 = 4. That cannot be different unless something in the equation is different.

On a side note, many similar kinds of stimuli produce corresponding outcomes. This information is important because we may link behaviours or feelings to similar stimuli under certain conditions. It helps us to influence a behaviour we want by providing certain stimuli under set conditions. Because we always have feelings, we may not always be consciously aware of them. Our feelings influence the processing of other stimuli, but we are not necessarily aware of that fact. For example, someone wearing a dark hat with a long dark beard and long black hair may have frightened us at one time when we were very young. For years, all has gone well, then, while walking alone on a poorly lit street one evening, from a small side street comes a person walking towards us wearing a dark hat and with a long dark beard and long black hair. Suddenly, we feel extreme fear. We believe that it is because we are alone, the street is poorly lit, and the person looks menacing. In fact, the emotions go back to the time when we were young and were frightened by a person wearing a dark hat. To be consciously aware of those feelings is a different level of awareness; it means to be aware that we are aware and consciously know that our present fear is a direct result of our past and as such is part of the brain processes, contributing to the terror we are experiencing in the present moment.

Awareness

I will use the following example to clarify what I mean by "being aware that we are aware." When driving on the highway we are responding to current traffic conditions. In other words, we are aware of those conditions but not necessarily aware that we are aware. That kind of awareness takes us another step deeper into our awareness. We will talk more about it in Chapter 5. For now, I will say that the complex processes of a multitude of stimuli contribute to the choices we make and a change in those stimuli and/or the brain processes of those stimuli produces a different outcome resulting in a different choice and thus a different behaviour. After I was asked whether I believed I had free will, I was on my way, not to develop a collection of thoughts expressed in a different way, but to discover a model that I call Procirclism.

CHAPTER 3
THE PROCIRCLISTIC MODEL: PROCIRCLISM

After thinking about our decision-making process and influences (stimuli) that contribute to—if not determine—the choices we make because of our brain processes and protocols regulating these processes, it was time to give a name to the model that had gradually unfolded in my mind. I wanted the name of my concept to reflect how our decisions and behaviours develop. This shape has a form which follows a process, and that process repeats itself without producing the same outcomes. It is called Procirclism, or the procirclistic model.

Procirclism is formed from two words, each an integral part of the concept. The brain processes stimuli that manifest in behaviour. Pro comes from the word *process*. Circl comes from the word *circle*: the circle, or cycle of stimuli being processed by the brain, producing repeating outcomes that become stimuli and are processed again with other stimuli, thus producing more outcomes. The procirclistic model deals with our behaviour, including the choices we make. It is based on the brain's processing of all stimuli. Stimuli are everything that affects the brain and that are processed by the brain. Each brain is unique to the person and develops according to the instructions of DNA. It is a complex organ and the way it processes stimuli is far from being understood at this time.

When the embryo develops in the womb, the brain is part of that development. As it develops according to its DNA, it begins to receive and process stimuli. Stimuli can come from outside or from within the brain itself as a kind of a self-stimulating process from the moment the brain becomes active. It is important to understand that any stimulus that affects the brain does not have to be recognized by us and most often is not. The existence of stimuli that affect the brain is not subject to our ability to recognize it. It stands alone whether we recognize it or not. Its processing does not depend on whether we recognize it or not. The brain processes remain below the threshold of our awareness, meaning they are not pushed to our awareness screen and we are not aware of them. Nevertheless, these processes take place and produce outcomes that affect our behaviour. More importantly, these processes affect the further development of the brain and the way in which subsequent stimuli are processed. This complexity may explain why we are still unable to fully understand our behaviours. It leads me to say that all behaviour is predictable but cannot be predicted. This statement can be made because there is nothing random in the brain. Everything is organized, structured and regulated by a multitude of complex protocols. Thus, behaviour is predictable because if we were able to understand how each individual brain process produces an outcome and manifests this outcome in specific behaviours and how one brain process affects consequent processes, we would be able to predict behaviour. The immense complexity is beyond our understanding, which makes it impossible for us to predict all behaviours. The same stimuli would not affect each brain in the same way. Each brain is different, but the finest details remain still below the threshold of recognition. Yet, what cannot be recognized should not be ignored or treated as not existing.

If we go back far enough in history, we find a time when people were declared dead when they were still alive. The phrase "saved by the bell" originated from this time. It would allow a person waking up in their coffin to pull a cord that would sound a bell so they could get help.

Today, science makes regular discoveries about the functioning of the brain. There are many indicators that lead us in a direction few of us want to go. You may be wondering what that direction could possibly be. It is quite simple, it leads us to question how free we are in the choices we make or what we want to do. Most of us will say that we can do whatever we want. The German philosopher Arthur Schopenhauer once said, "Man can do what he wills but cannot will what he wills." That is an interesting and profound statement. It is a suggestion concerning our freedom to do what we want. Let me put it another way: "We can do what we want but what we want is no choice at all."

Let's assume for a moment that our brain makes those choices when it processes all the stimuli it receives. These brain processes produce what we will, which I refer to as outcomes. Following Arthur Schopenhauer's statement that man can do what he wants, but he cannot will what he wills, we can say, "This is what I want to do," but what I want to do is not willed by me. In other words, what I want is not determined by me but when it is determined I can do what I want because what I want has already been determined when I want to do it. The brain process of stimuli has produced an outcome and it is that outcome that we execute in behaviour; it is the outcome that we want to do. So, we can do what we want, but what we want is produced by brain processes we are not aware of and so it creates a feeling that we choose what we want. Not being able to choose what we want relates to the second part of Schopenhauer's statement when he says that "man cannot will what he wills."

Digging a little more deeply, we can say that none of us participates consciously in the brain's processing of the stimuli.

Since we are not aware of that process, it feels as if we do what we want to do when we execute the choice that is the result of the brain processes of stimuli. We can even say, "I know I can do different things, but I simply want to do this." No doubt it feels as though it is our choice. We recognize other possible choices we can make but do not choose any of them and that solidifies, in our mind, that we do what we want. Not for a moment do we consider that we cannot make any other choice than the one we make. I know that this is a hard pill to swallow for most of us.

Procirclism deals with just this. It is an approach not expressed in this manner before and its conclusion could be considered revolutionary. Its foundation is the idea that the brain processes all stimuli. The brain only processes the smallest increment it can process and that increment is called a stimulus. Each stimulus must reach a certain threshold for the brain to be able to process it. Processing of stimuli is not random. It follows a strict protocol and regulative instructions. When stimuli reach the brain, they affect it in various ways, and influence aspects of it which then affect future processes. Thus, if it were possible for the brain to receive two of the same stimuli, the outcome of the process of the second stimulus would not be the same as the first.

In real life, we generally talk with each other about our experiences and express ourselves through our perceptions, of which our feelings are an integral part. When we are told that a relative or dear friend has died, we feel sadness or shock. In the next moment, if we were to witness something that would normally seem funny to us, it would most likely not seem funny at all. Our grief has influenced our perception of the next moment. It goes much further than this because what seems important before the moment we received the devastating news no longer seems important.

We know under normal circumstances we cannot just walk away from our job. But, if we get a call that our young daughter has been involved in a serious car accident and we need to go to the hospital as soon as possible, it is not hard to imagine that some of us may do just that, even if we were not given permission to leave.

These are clear examples of how circumstances influence behaviour. Here is another example. You applied for several jobs and receive a call that you have been considered for a position and they will confirm it the next day. You are happy because it pays a little more and you like the job better. Later that afternoon you receive a call from another company. They offer you the position you applied for, the pay is more than the other company offered and you like this job even better. You eagerly accept the job. You call your friend to tell him the good news. He asks what company you are going to work for and when you give him the name he tells you that they are in financial trouble and about to close down. He also tells you where you can find out more information. You look into it and confirm that it is true. Based on this new information you decline to take the job you had already accepted and take the first one when they give you a confirmation call the next day. However, you examine that company to find out whether they are reliable and solid. The experience with the other company has caused you to be more cautious when you might otherwise not have been. It is easy to follow how your behaviour was influenced by the information you received from your friend. For you to have taken the second, higher-paying job, you would have had to perceive what your friend told you about that company differently. If you did not believe what your friend said about that company because he often lied or changed information, then you might have taken the higher-paying job. Or perhaps you could have wanted it so badly that you ignored all the warning signs and took it anyway.

One thing is sure, the reason why you declined the better-paying job could not be the same reason you took that job, had you taken it. For that to be true it would mean that 2 + 2 = 4 (taking the job) and 5 (not taking the job). In this case, for the outcome to be 5 (not taking the job) we cannot use 2 + 2 because the outcome would remain 4 and we want 5.

A Peak into Perception

We will discuss perception in Chapter 7; however, I do want to briefly refer to it here. What the brain perceives is not necessarily factual. A person who is colorblind may not see the true essence of a red flower. In that case, the stimulus of red is not processed as red but filtered (in a manner of speaking) and processed as the brain perceives it. Such is also the case when we are told something, see, or experience something. We generally assume that what we see is the same as what any other person sees. Expressing the stimuli in numerical value we would say it is 2 + 2 but that may not be true. Perception comes into play and may alter these values which will result in different outcomes. Thus, our brain processes information (stimuli) as it perceives it and not as it is presented. What we were told does not remain as it is told but changes according to our perception. That perception may vary slightly or a great deal. For this reason, if everything is the same, then the outcome is also the same.

The very moment we do something or don't do something, it is exactly what we want to do at that moment. What we do is always what we want to do even when we say afterwards that we did not want to do it. It is just a verbal statement that states we are aware there were other choices and perhaps the one we made was not the right one. After having made a choice that was not the right one, we say that is because the outcome of the brain process produced the choice. As soon as we become aware of it, it makes us feel as if we did the choosing; stimuli are immediately produced and processed. It happens at lightning-fast speeds and new brain processes produce new outcomes. Such an outcome could be manifested when we say, "I don't think that was a good choice. I could have done this or that, but I didn't."

Outcomes as Manifested Behaviours

For instance, I am asked whether I want to buy that car. I have tested it, like it, and am thinking about it. The salesperson gives me a final discount. I decide not to buy the car. A moment later I regret that choice because after thinking about it for a moment I realize I had found no other place with the same car for the same price I was just given. There is no doubt that I am convinced this is what happened and that I chose to decline the offer and then chose to accept I made a mistake. That is how it feels to me and for that purpose to any one of us when we make choices. What we are not aware of is the working of our brain. Not one of us is aware of neurons flying through our brain and that communication among different parts of our brain is taking place. Yet that is happening and the choices we make as well as the behaviour we manifest are directly related to the outcomes of brain processes. When I decided not to buy the car, it felt as though I had made that choice and then acknowledged that I had made an error. I feel that I wanted to make the choice and I wanted to admit I was wrong. It felt that I did it because I wanted to and felt free from any coercion, pressure or other force to make those two choices. That is how we as human beings function, and we are not meant to avoid taking responsibility for our actions even when we have much less control than we think.

Taking responsibility is the result of brain processes and the outcomes it produces are stimuli that affect other brain processes and as such, our behaviour. How it feels to us is not how it happens. How can we recognize something we are not even aware of? The answer is not easily found nor is it easily understood; it is deeply hidden. It is subject to the process I am talking about. It lies in the essence of Procirclism and everything written in this book. We often have preconceived ideas which make it difficult for novel ideas to gain a foothold. It is as if new ideas must meet certain qualifications. It is understandable that we hold on to what is familiar to us. Novel ideas require an open approach and stand on their own merit. Just as a stranger cannot enter a home if the door is closed, so a novel idea cannot gain a foothold without an open mind. For new ideas to be welcomed, boundaries must be broken down.

Reading this book will provide stimuli to the brain that, after being processed, will produce a host of outcomes. These stimuli are mixed with our preconceived ideas, emotions, beliefs, doubts, fears, etc., all of which are also stimuli when activated. Whether we believe something to be true or false, these are manifestations of the outcome of brain processes. When we become consciously aware of that belief or non-belief, the belief may instantly change. In other words, we may instantly change from non-believing to believing or the other way around, such is the result of reactive stimuli that are produced at the instant we become aware of our belief or non-belief.

What We Do is What We Want to Do

It is difficult to accept that no matter what we do it is always what we want to do otherwise we could not have done it. We do it because our brain processes produce outcomes that reach the threshold of manifestation, meaning it is expressed in our behaviour. If someone holds a gun against our head and tells us to hand over our wallet and we do it, it means that we want to do it. Later we may say that we did not want to do it, but that is impossible. What we are trying to say is that we would have preferred not to have given our wallet but the fear of losing our life left us no choice. In fact, the brain processed all the stimuli and produced an outcome that manifested in behaviour. That behaviour was giving the wallet to the person with the gun. If we had not handed over the wallet, something else would have needed to be different. Perhaps it would have been not believing he would kill us. Perhaps we had specific training for these kinds of situations and knew how to disarm the person with little chance of getting injured and we were confident we could do this. The brain would have processed all that information and a different outcome would have resulted.

When we manifest behaviour, which includes spoken language, it instantly returns stimuli back to the brain at tremendous speed. Sometimes it leads to a change in our behaviour. In other words, if at one moment we decide to go shopping and then change our mind, there will be a change in our behaviour and we will feel as if we decided to change our mind freely without any apparent reason, force, pressure or manipulation. That is also how it appears to others.

I Call it Procirclism

As you have read, I call my model Procirclism. There are different models that relate to our will and freedom of our will. Some have mentioned determinism as a model. In Procirclism, nothing is determined and everything happens as it does because it could not have happened differently unless something else was different. What happens, whether it is events or human behaviour, does not happen because it is predetermined, nor does it happen because it is the effect of a cause. Procirclism is based on the process of stimuli. It cannot work without this process taking place in our brains. The brain does not know what will happen tomorrow nor do any one of us. When we drop a sheet of paper from the top balcony of a ten-storey building, it will turn and twist while falling. The wind will take it, and when it rains, the raindrops will push it down, and eventually it will fall on the ground. If we were to immediately take a picture before it moved again, we would see the spot. That sheet of paper did not fall there because it was determined to fall there nor was it the result of a single cause. We could try numerous times to drop a sheet of paper from the same balcony but most likely it would not land at the same spot as the first sheet of paper. Some of the factors that influenced where the sheet of paper landed the first time include the weight of the paper, the location from where the sheet of paper was dropped, the wind speeds and variations, where raindrops hit the sheet of paper, the size of the paper, and much more. For another sheet of paper to land at the same spot and for us to predict it, everything must be the same down to its smallest increment.

The same principle, although much more complicated, applies to our behaviour. When we see a car on the road that was involved in a car accident, it would be nearly impossible to recreate the same accident with the same damage, injuries (if there were any) and positions of the cars involved in the accident (if more than one car was involved). To recreate that accident with the same outcome all contributing factors would have to be the same.

Outcomes Are Always Perfect

In our daily lives, we may know what we wish would happen or we may plan for something to happen but none of us knows what will happen. Therefore, when a spaceship is launched and everything goes as planned then in general terms it happens as planned. Why did it happen that way? Not because it was planned but because all factors affecting the launch fell into place. The factors were known and anticipated and consequently what happened became predictable to the extent that everything had to go as foreseen. When we look at the details, we can ask, for example, to what extent the exact trajectory was known or anticipated as happened. We often say that planning can make things happen, but it never does. Through planning, a greater chance may be created for certain conditions to be present that are necessary to produce a desired outcome. Yet, whatever the outcome, it is always perfect, which must not be confused with desirable. When our planning failed to produce the conditions necessary to produce a desired outcome, the outcome produced is still perfect because it is the only possible outcome that could be produced by the process of stimuli;

therefore, it is perfect. When it comes to our brain, it does what it is designed to do: process stimuli. It keeps us alive. It ensures that our heart keeps pumping blood through our body, that the food we eat is being digested, that we keep breathing, etc.

Now we will look at the approach to our behaviour, our will, and freedom of our will, from a new angle. The question of whether we have free will or not has been discussed since the beginning of time. Great thinkers have participated in this debate, directly or indirectly, including Aristotle, David Hume and William James.

Procirclism is a dynamic process. It is changing constantly but not randomly. This process is not based on chance. When we begin to look at the alternatives to Procirclism, we encounter several difficulties which will be discussed in the chapters to come.

CHAPTER 4

I

What is I?

When hearing the statement, "I have to choose where to go on my next holidays," I ask myself who or what is doing the choosing? What is the "I" that does the choosing?

What is *I*? When we enter this sentence in a Word document and do a spelling and grammar check, it will correct the sentence and suggest replacing *is* with *am*. The sentence would change to "What am I?" We normally don't ask, "What is I?" I am positive that you would agree and probably suggest that "Who am I?" sounds more appropriate to us.

Well that is precisely what I don't want to ask and answer. I want to ask, "What is *I*?" Can you answer that question? If you try, you will probably change the question to "Who am I?" and begin describing who you are. If I were to ask you, "What is wood?" you would most likely describe what wood is and give a definition. That is what I want for *I*. Every time we say, "I choose to watch football over basketball," or, "I want to buy a new house," we use the word "I." In that case, "I" identifies you or me.

Years ago, I asked a teenager, "Who are you?" He began saying his name. I stopped him and asked whether he would still be him if he had a different name. He laughed and said yes. I asked the question again, "Who are you? I would like to know who you are." He continued by describing his physical attributes to which I responded, "So if you lose an arm, you are not you anymore because you just said that your arms, legs, face, hair and feet are you?" He laughed a little awkwardly, and I sensed he did not think it was funny anymore. We went on for a few more minutes and then he stopped, looked at me and said loudly, "I don't know who I am anymore."

Let's think about this for a moment. Who I am is different from the question "What is I?" I is I as is, without attributes and descriptive elements. No, it is not a typing error. I did not want to say, "I am who I am." I deliberately said, "I is I as is." I mean it in the sense that the tree is as it is with the only difference being that the tree has attributes. When you read my definition of *I* it may become clearer. As long as *I* is, it is as is. There are no specific conditions for *I* to be *I*. In this case I am talking about the *I* that makes the choices and for the purpose of this book, that is different from the I that identifies me as being me—with my attributes—and nobody else.

When we talk about potato soup, we know that when we take the potatoes out of the soup it is not potato soup anymore. When we say I, it is as is, and nothing can be taken away from this I for it not to be as is anymore. Potato soup is descriptive, which means that it describes the soup and tells us something about the soup. *I* does not do this; it is not descriptive at all. In a complex way, it simply states I, and therefore is as is without any required qualifications to be *I*. There is only one exemption. *I* is no longer *I* when *I* is no more. *I* is no more when the brain cannot realize itself anymore, through awareness. When we are brain-dead, *I* is no more. When self-awareness is gone—the brain cannot realize itself anymore through awareness when it normally could and did while we are not brain dead as certain functions to sustain life are still performed—*I* is no more. It is extremely important to know the definition of *I* as written in this book. Without that definition, everything will seem confusing because the general understanding of I is quite different and when applied in that sense, Procirclism is difficult to understand. It can be confusing in our daily life because when we use the word "I" and refer to it as the *I* that decides or chooses behaviour, we cannot explain what does the choosing and how or where it is done. Although not mentioned, *I* is involved in the procirclistic model, and without a clear understanding of *I* as presented in this book, Procirclism cannot be understood as it is meant. In fact, without *I*, Procirclism has no life. When we ask what is doing the choosing, we must define *I* because most of us have likely said at one time, "I am doing the choosing and deciding" when talking about ourselves as the one who decides and chooses.

Not Who but What Does the Choosing

It is not easy to grasp because we don't pay it much attention. We often say that we did this or that but never really think about the question: What does something? When we say, "I decided not to go to the movies," the "I" that decided not to go to the movies must be something that we can see, something concrete, an entity as it performs an activity, choosing. If it is there, it must be the *I* that directs the brain to perform an action because the brain is involved in all we do. Can we imagine that I (as we identify ourselves with) decide or choose, and must therefore tell the brain what to do, and then the brain acts upon that. Is that what we believe is happening when we say "I choose," or "I will?" In that case something must exist outside the brain and instruct the brain what to do? It is up to you to find it and explain how it works if you believe it works that way. Here is another question that must be answered: What is the process that decides what we want and how the brain is being instructed to manifest what we want? Nothing happens without the involvement of our brain. Confused? Following this path can only lead to confusion because when trying to explain it, we run into brick walls.

We use I, when we say, for example, "I am thinking," or, "I am eating," and as a result we can easily identify who is eating and observe the activity of eating. But it does not answer the question: What is it that does the choosing and how does the process work?

When we say, "I am choosing to turn right," we can observe the result of that choice, but we cannot observe the making of the choice itself and where it is made unless we can identify what does the choosing and where it takes place. We manifest the outcomes of all choices in our behaviour.

The unresolved challenge for us is to prove, with certainty, when we say, "I choose," that "I" (as you use it to identify yourself as not being anybody else but you) that is choosing is also an entity outside of the brain and directs the brain to perform the action necessary for us to manifest the choice I made (my arms, legs, hair etc. cannot do any choosing but are part of the identification of me when I say, "I choose"). Only when we can prove that I (as we use it to identify ourselves with) also exists as an independent entity that directs the brain to manifest our choices, can we answer the question, What does the choosing? However, I believe you will have an extremely difficult time proving this. There is a reason why the answer to this question is not yet answered. Most of us have never asked that question and perhaps think it is simply ridiculous. Only if we delve deep into our decision-making process will this question become the most obvious question to ask. The simple answer, "I choose," does not even come close.

Then Something Unfolded in My Mind

At first glance, it may seem confusing but when pondering this idea with intensity and persistency, some logic will appear. The difficulty is being able to accept what unfolds. What unfolded for me was not a preconceived idea for which I am trying to find supportive arguments, but I discovered building blocks that seamlessly fit, one upon the other, and resulted in a conclusion I could not have imagined at the outset. To have an idea and then try to support it is going backwards, or thinking from the top down. I wanted to go from the bottom up and let what unfolded take the lead in its own essence without trying to fit it into a preconceived idea. Procirclism is the result of years of persistent pondering and thinking about these issues. What resulted was as much a surprise to me as it may be for you as you read this.

At this point it seems useless to continue unless we address the *I* and define it. The most common understanding of I and how it is being defined by most of us is to describe by asking who I am. When the question, "What is I?" is asked, we default to our standard answer to the question: Who am I? That is not what is being asked here. When we say, "I am choosing," we need to know what is doing the choosing. When we can define *I* (the *I* that does the choosing), we have a better understanding of the *I phenomenon*. The definition of *I* is therefore extremely important in the free will debate. It is also a major factor in Procirclism. The essence of *I* has not been discovered, recognized, seen, located or presented to us as an independent physical entity. It is not the I that I mention when I am describing myself as I, meaning nobody else.

It can be interesting to ponder the question: Who am I? In fact, when we say that is my arm, my face, my hair or my leg, it simply means that these belong to me. We routinely say, "That's my thought, my opinion, my car." To whom does it belong? In this scenario, we clearly make a distinction between I (as we use it to identify ourselves) and thought, object or opinion. All three belong to me but are not *I* (that what does the choosing). Unless we can define *I*, we will encounter enormous problems when we discuss the free will issue. If I say, "I have free will," then I must know what is free and how free will works as opposed to a will that is not free. Therefore, we must also define will. "It is my will to do that," signifies a problem we are facing. "I" and "will" are not the same, otherwise we would be unable to say, "It is my will to do that," because it suggests that I possess that will, and therefore I can say it is my will. If I say that "This is my car," nobody would question whether there is a distinction between "I" and "car," and nobody would think that "I" and "car" are the same. It is not even a question.

If we delve a bit further, we may reach the point where we assume that the *I* is unlocatable. It is a matter of opinion whether there is even an *I* that resides somewhere, is an independent entity, or can be located as such. If there is, does it reside in our body? Can it be seen? Is it matter or an organ like our heart or brain? So far, we have been unable to locate it or see it and it has not been defined, yet we consistently express what it does when we say, "I think," "I changed my mind," "I doubted that," "I did not know that," etc. For most of us, whatever *I* is, it seems to do what it wants, and that is exactly how it feels to most of us; it seems to make all the choices, as in, "I decided to do that."

It does what it wants, but we have no idea how it is doing it, where it takes place and whether we can observe the *I*. No matter how we twist or turn it, what seems so normal to us and is generally accepted by cultures all over the world, suddenly does not seem to be so simple anymore. We need to define *I* to come to a better understanding of whether *I* is a power that rules our brain and operates independently or whether such an *I* exists at all.

I have tried to define *I* for a long time. Continually asking myself who I am suddenly made me realize that I had to ask a different question regarding the choices we make. When I say, "I decide to take a vacation," it is obvious that I am talking about me (I) as opposed to anybody else. However, I needed to know *what* decides. To know what decides, I needed to know the definition of *I* because we have said, are saying, and will continue to say: "I choose to go for a walk." Since it cannot be the identifying I that does the choosing, I had to define *I* to be able to explain what is truly happening while at the same time it must accommodate the expression, "I decide to buy that car." In other words, finding a definition for *I* that on the surface does not change anything while under the surface everything changes.

Gradually I started to recognize that there couldn't be an independent *I*. We all know that if surgeons remove the brain from our skull we will die. It is well known that the brain controls our muscles for our arms, legs and hands to move; our brain does the work. If the brain is damaged so that our right arm cannot move, I would not be able to reverse that problem. For us to run, our brain and muscles must all be working in a certain manner to make this happen. I cannot run backwards when the brain is working on running forwards. I—or any one of us—cannot consciously adjust the working of the brain in such a way that I start running backwards when it wants to go forward. When our car is in the drive position, something happens mechanically with the car that makes it go forward when we push the accelerator. It is impossible for the car to move backwards because the gears are lined up to go forward; the gears must shift in such a position (R) so that the car goes backwards when pressing the accelerator.

So, when we say, "I choose to go on vacation," it clearly means that I choose and no one else. We can ask ourselves whether the "I" that represents the person who goes on vacation is also the "*I*" that makes the choice. Did you notice that the first "I" used in the previous sentence relates to who and the second "*I*" relates to what. That signifies a dual meaning of the essence of *I*, which we are normally not even thinking about or aware of. It is the direct result of the type of question we ask: "What does the choosing?" When I go on vacation it is I, as others know me, recognize me, see me, who is going on vacation. However, that cannot be the *I* that does the choosing. When we want to point at the location where the act of choosing takes place we are unable to find it in my hands, feet or legs. Yet when we say I, our physical body and other attributes are all part of I. Thoughts like these require a workable solution. *I* must be defined.

I Defined

After thinking about this for some years, I came up with the following definition of *I* as in, *I choose*.

I is the self-realization of the brain through awareness.

The brain's own process is the cause of us becoming aware. Whatever is pushed to our awareness screen, we become aware of. It is not the result of a decisive action where I decide to become aware of something. Being aware happens. Yet, we are not always consciously aware of everything. Awareness is just another dimension of our brain, and as mentioned before, when we become aware of something it is immediately affected by our awareness and therefore processed again. This can lead to the times when we decide to change our mind. It feels as if we decide to change our mind while, at the moment of awareness, that which we become aware of is instantly reprocessed, which produces another outcome. When that outcome is manifested, it can happen in the form of "I change my mind." Awareness is required for the brain to realize itself so that I can say, "I think." The brain does the thinking. When we say, "I think," it does not happen anywhere other than in the brain. The brain does the processing. It pushes itself to the awareness screen and *I* happens, as in, "I decide to take a holiday." I, in the sense that it is an independent entity that chooses at will, does not exist. Yet it surely feels as if we are in full control and can change our mind at will.

Then what is *I* that does the choosing? The brain, this most complex organ, realizes itself and uses one of its phenomenal qualities, awareness, to do this. When it does, the *I* that chooses appears and we can say, "I choose to do that," but the choice represents the outcome of the brain process. When we say, "I choose to do that," we imply that, somehow, I could also have chosen not to have done that. That is just not true. All stimuli and other factors used in the process, result in a particular outcome. Without anything being different, the process will produce the same outcome, thus the same choice will be made. In simple terms 2 + 3 + 4 + 5 = 14 and it will always be 14. We cannot say sometimes it is 15 or 16 or any other number than 14. To get a different outcome we must at least change one of the four numbers that are being added. We have discussed this on previous pages.

Without awareness, I believe we cannot realize *I am I*. Awareness allows us to say things such as, "I am aware of the car coming my way," or, "I was not aware of it, if I was, I would not have done it." A number of pages back we have seen that the decision-making process also uses I when we say, "I choose not to go." It is the meaning of I in that sentence that needs to be defined when we want to indicate what is making the decision and where this process happens. That *"I"* is not the same that identifies me as not being any other person. The identifying I describes me and is visible, as me, to others. That I is not the thinking *I*, but the descriptive I. That I does not indicate in any way what is doing the thinking. Here is where awareness comes into the picture to define *I* as in "I choose to leave." Without awareness, life would be very different. We are human beings who are aware or at least can be aware. Therefore, when the brain uses that awareness to realize itself, we can say: "I think" or "I choose," and based on the definition (*I* is the self-realization of the brain through awareness, expressed as I) it is the brain that does the thinking.

In our daily language, the I's are merged, and after having defined *I* (as in "I choose"), it does not create a conflict. One describes I as not being anyone else, and the second *I* indicates what does the choosing. This can only be done when we apply the definition I have just given. Without that definition, we are back to square one and the merging of the I's is senseless. Both require awareness to be realized. Without awareness, there is no I that identifies me from anybody else. Without awareness, everything just is, almost in a robotic sense where robots may be able to recognize things but are not consciously aware of this. That process is simply mechanical; the brain does the thinking and choosing, and through awareness it realizes the physical appearance that is attached to I. In a sense, we could say, "I becomes aware of the physical body it travels in through life" and through *I*, awareness of me as being *I* becomes possible. Now, when I talk about "I choose," it is understood that my brain chooses and manifests such through my physical attributes. Since it is my brain it also identifies me as not being any other person. However, without the definition of *I*, as given earlier, this is not possible. It would mean that when people say, "I choose," they mean that who they are chooses and has freedom of choice. We discussed that stimuli are processed in the brain and produce outcomes. Those outcomes, when reaching the threshold, are manifested in behaviour. The I that identifies me and includes my voice, ears, hair, arms and legs is different from the *I* that does the thinking. The I that describes me answers the question: Who am I? The *I* that makes the choices answers the question: What makes the choices? When we say, "I can do whatever I want," it sounds and feels as if I am saying that I, not you or anybody else, can do whatever I want and you cannot stop me or change what I want. In this sense, I is void of a definition that says what it is rather than who it is. Knowing who chooses does not give us a clue as to what chooses, how it chooses or where the choosing takes place. To answer that question, we needed to define *I*.

The brain does not sit in our skull and suddenly decide we should get up and start running or buy an airline ticket to a foreign country. That sounds kind of ridiculous, doesn't it? In fact, we may ask whether there is anything that can do as it wants and is void of any knowable or unknowable reason for whatever is done or not done. Without the processing of stimuli, whether external or internal, the brain does not produce outcomes. Only when we recognize *I* as the self-realization of the brain through awareness, expressed as *I*, does it make sense when we say "I choose," but that *I* is not free to choose what it wants. In fact, it cannot want anything;

it processes stimuli to produce outcomes as I mentioned earlier. It produces the only outcomes that can be produced when certain stimuli are processed in a certain manner. Nevertheless, it feels as if I have full control and can change my decision as I please. In my opinion it is just an illusion. There is no I that is a standalone independent entity with power and knowledge that can do what it wants, void of any influential stimuli of any kind. In essence, I in that sense, does not and cannot exist. The I that identifies me as not being you or that person or any other person is not an independent entity, nor can it be. It is enveloped in the definition of *I* where it is the self-realization of the brain through awareness and that awareness reaches into our physical existence as we become aware of it.

Because of the complexity of this *I phenomenon*, and because it is a central point in Procirclism, I will shed some light on the thinking process behind it. When I say, "I am thinking," the following question can be asked. What does the thinking? The answer is the brain (the brain realizes itself through awareness, expressed as *I*). Then there is I that distinguishes me from any other person. However, when we define *I* as the self-realization of the brain through awareness, it also reaches into the awareness of our physical body. This means that awareness is required to realize who we are as a recognizable being. To be able to identify me as I, we must first determine what *I* is because it also makes choices and decisions, expressed as "I choose," or "I decide." Thus, when *I* is defined as the self-realization of the brain through awareness, we created a basis where *I* is extended to our physical being through awareness.

Awareness provides an opportunity for the brain to realize itself. When it does so, it becomes *I*, but in this case, *I* is the self-realization of the brain through awareness, expressed as *I*. I have come at this from different angles and have done so repeatedly because it is essential in the procirclistic model. We can make the comparison of looking in a mirror and seeing ourselves. The brain does kind of the same thing. It realizes itself through awareness instead of the mirror. Without a mirror, we don't see ourselves, and without awareness the brain cannot realize itself. Like the brain, we are still here even without the mirror and the brain still functions even without awareness. When the brain realizes itself through awareness, it distinctively expresses *I* as in "I am thinking," indicating what does the thinking—the brain—rather than who does it. When we talk about us, in terms of the persons who manifest behaviour, it makes sense that each of us is a unique vehicle through which the outcomes of brain processes are expressed as behaviour. My hands, feet and eyes all require brain processes to function, and function with purpose. In that sense, our behaviour is always in perfect harmony with the outcome of brain processes. It is a matter of preferences or ideology when we evaluate something as good or bad, perfect or imperfect.

Any outcomes of brain processes expressed in behaviour are always perfect because the outcomes could not have been different unless something in the processing was also different. When we play a soccer match and accidentally score in our own goal, we say, that is not perfect. Yet it is a perfect goal. If the score remains 1-0 for the other team, they have a perfect win. It is a perfect game with a perfect outcome, the perfect result of every single event in the game. The game, having gone this way, was not the desired outcome for the losing team. Yet it is a perfect outcome. Perfection in this example is meant in the sense that the game could not have ended differently unless something different would have happened during the game. The difference could have been something like not scoring in their own goal, or the ball not taking that sudden bounce and hit the player's knee from where it rolled in their own goal. However, this game like any other can only produce one outcome. That is the perfect outcome. That outcome is different from any desired outcome. The difference is that there can be many different desired outcomes but there is always, only one perfect outcome.

The Choices Are Always Perfect

For a behaviour to be different, the brain processing must be different. A carbon copy of a certain brain process cannot produce a different outcome (behaviour) than the original brain process nor a different behaviour. Thus, our behaviour in that sense, is always perfect because it is the only behaviour that could be produced, as an outcome, by that brain process. When we say, "I am making a decision," it is the brain that makes the decision. It does so as it processes stimuli and produces outcomes. Those outcomes are manifested in our behaviour when they reach the behaviour threshold. What is manifested may feel as if it is the result of our conscious choice, but it is not determined by an independent entity called I. There is no such I. An independent I does not exist and cannot exist as mentioned before. However, it certainly feels as if I decide.

When we say, "I decided," we believe that we decided, and it definitely feels that way. As the definition states: *I* is the self-realization of the brain through awareness. The brain is the place where the action happens, where information and/or stimuli are being processed and outcomes produced at enormous speeds This definition is evolved from necessity, from the bottom up. After it has unfolded in this manner, it is hard to imagine that I can be anything different such as an independent entity that directs what the brain does. Yet it still is extremely complex and will cause many to shake their heads. The self-realization of the brain that presents itself through awareness feels to us like I, the reason we say, "I decide." We are simply not conscious of the processes that take place. The making of decisions, when it happens at a conscious level, feels to us as if we are weighing the pros and cons and making conscious decisions. In fact, none of us decide in the sense of having the option to make any other decision at the very instance one decision is made. When outcomes are presented to our awareness, immediate communication takes place in our brain. Awareness immediately influences outcomes as stimuli produced by awareness are instantly sent back and processed at incredible speeds, producing another outcome that is presented to our awareness screen. We are never consciously aware of this process, but it feels to us as if we have thought about it. The new outcome reaches our awareness screen and it feels as if I made the new decision. It feels, and we experience it, as if we looked at the pros and cons and decided to make this decision. There is no arguing with how it feels to us. Only when we ask specific questions and delve much deeper into the decision-making process does this incredible phenomenon unfold—what I call Procirclism. There is no I outside of the *I* definition that does the processing or considers the pros and cons because *I* is not an entity and has never been seen, located or discovered. The definition of *I* states that it is the self-realization of the brain through awareness. *I* is in fact the brain but feels as if it is me, I.

Behaviour... Choice or Process

When toddlers are playing together and we watch them, they just continue with what they are doing. Not until they realize their parents are watching them do they change. That is what happens when outcomes are presented to our awareness screen. At lightning speed, stimuli produced at the instant of awareness are sent back, processed, and without realizing any of this we suddenly change our behaviour and believe it is the result of what we want to do, while in fact it is the manifestation of the outcome of the brain process. Outcomes that reach the awareness threshold appear on our awareness screen and it seems we are making a conscious choice while in fact we observe the brain in action by the appearance of outcomes of its processes without realizing the brain process took place. Nothing changes because, either way, we do what we do and don't do what we do not do. Why then, is it of any importance to know why we do what we do? I believe that understanding and accepting this will help us to gradually become more aware of influences that affect our behaviour. In that sense, behaviour is the result of process rather than choice. Commercials are based on this, election campaigns use it, and people use it every day. Many atrocities have happened because of stimuli that have been processed by the brain, in the procirclistic manner, and produced outcomes, sometimes painful ones.

Approaching this from the point of view that all behaviours are just a matter of choice and we could have made a different choice if we had wanted to, ignores the evidence that our decisions are not a matter of choice when we defend them by providing reasons for what we did. It also ignores the fact that influential factors such as violent video games, online radicalization, validating a young child, demonstrating respect and integrity, honesty, gossip, bullying, abuse and neglect, and the daily stream of news that reaches our brain affect our behaviour. For some it may be less and for others more.

On the other hand, when we approach it differently and accept that all influences affect us, varying from mild to severe, we can change undesired behaviours by changing the stimuli we expose ourselves to. Remember, this is not a conscious decision but a result of stimuli, for example, the stimuli caused by reading this book. Our brain may be affected by it so that it starts craving more knowledge about this. Our brain may start asking questions and it feels as if we are asking questions such as why am I doing this, or believing that or feeling this way? We need to use the same concept (Procirclism) to bring about change. I would likely never have written this book if I had not been asked that question more than thirty years ago. It was a stimulus that activated my brain and surely felt as if I decided to find answers. It still feels like that and will most likely never change, but it does not take away the fact that it happens because of stimuli that is processed by my brain.

The Difficulty with the Counter Argument

I will briefly continue with my argument that it is a daunting task to insist there is an independent I that does the choosing freely, randomly, and has the brain at its full disclosure, waiting to be instructed to manifest behaviours. For argument's sake let us assume there is an independent I that performs the act of choosing. When we believe that pros and cons are being used in a decision-making process, then they must be stored and processed somewhere. Next the pros and cons are being looked at, weighed, and being used, either by inclusion or exclusion, to make a choice. Of course, many more factors contribute to the choices being made. All this must take place somewhere. When *I* has come up with a decision it must be manifested. Remember, we are still talking about an independent *I*. The choice made can only be manifested with the assistance of our brain. Thus, somehow the brain must be organized in such a manner that the choice being made is exactly manifested as chosen. In our assumption, only I can do that. This means, that the independent *I*, which we cannot locate nor observe, is instructing the brain to perform the choice it made. There is no human being on this planet that has ever consciously experienced that an independent *I* is organizing the brain to perform a choice I made. If it is unimaginable for just one choice, how much more impossible must it be for a continuity of choices that must be manifested, and the brain organized, for this to happen continuously?

By now, it has become clear that in a model that assumes there is an independent *I*, *I* must be observable, have the capacity to obtain or store information and then process it. This has never been proven. An independent *I* that does the choosing has never been substantiated as a working model. On the other hand, the brain has been substantiated. If we cannot explain how *I* works nor are able to describe what it is and cannot confirm that it is matter, such as an organ that can store information, it becomes difficult to believe that I can do whatever I want, in the sense of free will.

The procirclistic model seems more plausible, as the definition of *I* (the self-realization of the brain through awareness) fits seamlessly into this model. There is no independent force that directs the brain regarding what to do, and it is even harder to imagine that such a force exists and is the *I force* as in, "I decide what I want." In our daily expressions, we already recognize there is more to our decision-making process than simple will. As I have indicated, we often say, "If I had known, I would not have done that," or, "I did not have a choice," or, "I based my decision on the wrong information," and we can go on and on. In court, during a murder trial, the prosecution attempts to establish a motive for the murder. It suggests they want to convince the jury that no murder is committed simply because someone desired to murder another person without a reason, cause, force or any other known or unknown contributing factor. Recognizing that factors play a role in the decision-making process, it is not difficult to imagine these factors must be processed somewhere. I say it is processed in the brain. The brain is a recognizable organ that can be located and many of its workings observed. For the *I do/choose what I want* believers, it has suddenly become an extremely difficult concept to defend.

First, as mentioned before, *I* cannot be located. If it exists, it must be an independent entity choosing independently from any influential factors or different options, which is not possible because, before it can do so, it must exist in one form or another. Next, it must be able to affect the brain so that it performs in such a manner that the choice *I* has made is manifested in behaviour. In this case, no complicated process is necessary as it is just one thing at a time such as "I turn right," or, "I go to the movies," and that command should set the brain in such a condition that it manifests that behaviour. This suggests that the brain is dormant until it is instructed to act by *I*. In other words, the *I* must be able to affect the brain to the point that it manifests behaviour according to the choice *I* has made. There is no evidence of this. If this were true (I, the independent entity, instructs the brain to manifest the complete free choice it made), no complicated process is necessary because it is just the manifestation of "I want to have a cup of coffee." We should never ask why because the freedom of choice is free of any influential factors, which is an oxymoron because there are no influential factors in total freedom of choice. The notion of influences is absurd in this concept.

A Touch of Science

It is well known that behaviour is complex. It simply cannot be a matter of choice without any influential factors because that would not be complex. There seems to be no place here for a statement like, "I can do what I want," unless we add that what we want to do is not a matter of free choice but of process and is as such already determined and therefore it is what we want. Some may suggest, in error, that this supports their belief in having free will. "I is not an independent physical entity and is not observable nor identifiable." I cannot think because it does not exist other than in the form of the self-realization of the brain through awareness. It is the brain that does the choosing, the processing of stimuli and much more. Popular contemporary research suggests that in a healthy brain, the amygdala (an almond-shaped structure in the brain that is essential for the processing of emotions, to feel certain emotions and to perceive them in other people) and the hippocampus (a small region of the brain that deals with the formation of long-term memory) work together so that emotional experiences are put into context. It is believed that the hippocampus develops more slowly than the amygdala. This affects brain processes and thus behaviour. The I, as an independent entity that directs these processes from the outside, is not involved in this at all because it is purely a brain-processing issue. The hippocampus is involved in making memories. When the hippocampus is not functioning as required (or supposed to, according to its function and purpose), it affects certain memories. Indirectly, this affects behaviour because of brain processes that produce different outcomes when the hippocampus functions as it is supposed to, rather than when it does not. Some say that the hippocampus is eventually destroyed in patients with Alzheimer's disease.

We know that chemicals are involved in brain processes. That means that an imbalance in brain chemicals affects brain processes, thus behaviour, in a different manner from when it is in balance. The prefrontal cortex seems to be an important factor in the development of one's personality. The prefrontal cortex is involved in decision making, expressions of personality, and moderating social behaviour. At no time is the I involved as in "I decide." It seems logical that the existence of an independent entity called I is most unlikely. On the other hand, it is also extremely difficult to imagine that an independent I does not exist because it feels so real. I decide. It seems that the feeling of independent choice is supported because we are not consciously aware of the brain processes that produce outcomes, which are manifested in behaviour. In addition, the belief that we make the decisions is ingrained in us when we say, "I decide," and rarely, if at all, say, "My brain decided." Yet, I as an independent entity does not and cannot exist, no matter how it feels to us. I is not an entity and has never been seen, located or identified.

There is no I involved in the statement "I can do whatever I want" unless what I (self-realization of the brain through awareness) want is what the brain produces as the outcome of a brain process. Its complexity is immense, but there is no alternative because it would require identifying the I that does the choosing and being able to locate it and observe its workings. This can only be done when I is the self-realization of the brain through awareness. If we assume there is an independent I, it means that we would be able to examine it for defects, illnesses and mutations. None of that can be done or even considered because it has never been discovered.

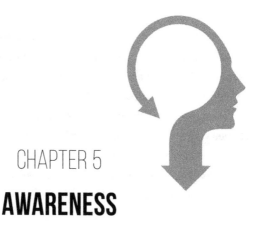

CHAPTER 5

AWARENESS

So far, I have briefly mentioned awareness without going into further details. Awareness is an integral part of our being. After we discussed and defined *I*, it is a smooth and logical transition to discuss awareness as an important factor of Procirclism. Before I am aware, I am not aware.

To describe awareness in Procirclism is to look at our awareness as a big empty computer screen. The screen is blank and ready to display content that the computer reveals on its screen. It is the output of a process that appears on the screen, which I call the awareness screen. It can be illustrated, for example, by the click of a mouse that causes data to appear on a computer screen when it is awakened from its sleeping state. Not until data becomes visible to us can we see it. When we look at it, we can react to it, work with it and much more. This is how we can visualize our awareness. We are not aware of something until it appears on our awareness screen. Anything that appears on this screen is the result of our brain processes. These processes happen at such speeds that we are not aware of them. This complicates things because when we are not aware of these processes we simply believe that we can will what we want, or in other words, we can do as we please.

Before we become aware, we are not aware. When we become aware, it is because our brain has pushed it onto that awareness screen. Before awareness can appear, it must reach the threshold of appearance, which I refer to as the threshold of awareness in Procirclism. Stimuli set the process in motion. At the same time, when something appears on the screen of our awareness, I is instantly present because *I* becomes aware of it. Awareness is directly linked to I because it produces *I* as the brain realizes itself through awareness (see definition of *I*). Could we also say that I without awareness does not exist?

> The definition of *I*: *I* is the self-realization of the brain through awareness and as such it is a representation of the brain, and is therefore not an independent entity. It does not, nor can it have independent powers or knowledge, neither can it make any decisions like "I choose." *I* does not and cannot exist as a stand-alone entity.

When we look at the definition it seems clear that *I* requires awareness because only through awareness can the brain realize itself, and when that happens, I happens. That is when you and I say "I." As we recognize from its definition, *I* is not an independent entity. The brain cannot realize itself without awareness in which case "I" would be absent.

The definition of I also allows us to understand why I is a representation of the brain through awareness. The key word is awareness. There it is, on our awareness screen. This means: no awareness, no vehicle for the brain to realize itself, thus no I. Without *I*, as defined, we would be here but unaware of our own existence. Yet awareness exists and, again, I refer to it as our awareness screen to which the brain pushes information that appears, in the form it does, on that screen. We are aware of what appears on the screen and we can say: "I know that I have a meeting at 11 a.m. this morning." From our previous argument, we may assume that I cannot exist independently. Thus, I was not involved in becoming aware of the appointment. We will talk about this a little further into this chapter when we discuss thoughts and memories. In the brain a process takes place, and the outcome, conditional upon many instructions that are embodied in the brain structure or its DNA, is pushed to our awareness screen, and as we become aware of it, it feels as if we are thinking about the 11 a.m. appointment. It is true, I am thinking about it from the moment it appears on my awareness screen. Because it happens at lightning speed we do not and cannot know that in milliseconds the information was pushed onto our awareness screen. Thus, we become aware of it as if we initiated thinking about it. That is how it feels as it appears on our awareness screen. At the very instant we become aware of it, the outcome may change. That change may be significant or so minor that we may not even notice it. As we become aware of something, feedback is instantly sent to the brain as stimuli, causing a new process that produces another outcome. When something reaches our awareness screen or when we become aware of it, it creates stimuli. These stimuli are processed and produce another outcome that is pushed to our awareness screen and is manifested through any kind of behaviour. To us, it feels as if we decide how we will behave and that we can change that behaviour, or our mind, at will.

We decide to go to the grocery store and then change our mind and decide to go later. When I am buying a cup of coffee, I suddenly think about a meeting I have this morning. The brain pushes that meeting to my awareness screen (this is caused by a trigger or stimulus of some kind and does not happen spontaneously) but it feels as if I am thinking about it. Pushing that meeting to my awareness screen does not happen randomly. It is the result of a complex process of stimuli. In other words, it is the reason I become aware of it. Furthermore, that is what happens when I become aware of my 11 a.m. appointment at the exact moment I do, to the second, and more precisely, to the fraction of a second. It may feel as if I am directing my awareness to my schedule for this morning but that does not mean it happens like that. As a matter of fact, it is impossible for that to happen, even when we feel it does. If something has triggered my attention to bring up the schedule for this morning, that is plausible. I don't think we imagine that nothing happened, known or unknown to us, and our schedule came to mind spontaneously. I can demonstrate this by asking why anything else did not come to mind and appear on my awareness screen. The fact that my schedule appeared and nothing else may reasonably suggest that something triggered this.

Being Consciously Aware

We don't usually ask how it would work when *I* directs my attention towards my schedule. The idea that I don't do the choosing seems so absurd that we never ask questions like: "What is I?" or "What do we actually mean when we say I choose?" or "What is will and awareness?" We may get confused when we ask what awareness is. How can we know so much but are aware only of small fragments and sometimes are not aware of anything at all? It feels so simple when we say, "I am aware of it." We all seem to know what we mean when we say this. Awareness is part of our humanity. However, we are only consciously aware of something when it appears on our *awareness screen.*

There is a difference between being aware and being aware that we are aware. When we are watching a movie, we are aware of the movie, yet we are probably not aware that we are aware of the movie, but realize that we are watching a movie. Some of us may never have gone that deep. We don't routinely say, "I am aware that I am watching this movie while sitting in this chair." When this happens, the brain is signalling that it is watching the movie, and this can only happen on the awareness screen when the *I* is a self-realization of the brain through awareness. Stimuli is processed and pushes this awareness of being aware to our awareness screen and we can say, "I am aware that I am aware I am watching the movie while sitting in this chair." We may have said, "As soon as I realized it, I changed my mind." That phrase shows that as soon as the brain pushes something to our awareness screen, it produces instant responsive stimuli that are as such processed by the brain and produce outcomes that are again pushed to our awareness screen and manifested through our behaviour as, "I changed my mind." We can look at our awareness as a weighing factor. As soon as we become consciously aware of something, that something intensifies. It has a greater impact. It weighs more and is instantly processed with the effect of the awareness factor that has changed it, thus producing a different outcome. We are completely ignorant of the process that took place from the millisecond we became aware of its outcome and the brain producing another outcome. When we become aware of that new outcome, we may say, "I changed my mind," and it certainly feels as if we changed our mind consciously and with purpose. This feeling is enhanced because we do not consciously experience the brain processes involved that produce outcomes which we execute through behaviour.

Once something appears on our awareness screen, we become aware of it and it instantly creates new stimuli, causing new brain processes to produce new outcomes, pushing more information to our awareness screen. We become aware of more but were not aware of it before this instant. I became aware of my 11 a.m. meeting this morning when buying a cup of coffee, and it led me to think about the kind of meeting it was; suddenly I knew that I still had to finish some notes for that meeting. While calling the secretary to ask her to type those notes, I realized that she was off today. It feels like I am now consciously scanning for possibilities to get the notes typed before I get to the meeting. It feels as if I am actively doing the thinking. However, after being processed, stimuli cause the brain to push something to my awareness screen. As soon as it reaches my awareness screen, it is sent as stimuli from that awareness screen and new brain processes begin. Sometimes fractions of what is pushed to my awareness screen (what I become aware of) produce reactive stimuli which are processed and their next manifestation may be linked to what was last on my awareness screen. For example:

> I become aware of a meeting > reactive stimuli > process > manifestation of outcome = I become aware of the fact I still need to prepare some notes for the meeting.

> In turn, that produces reactive stimuli at the moment it reaches my awareness screen > process > manifestation of outcome = I want to call the secretary to type the notes.

> This appears now on my awareness screen > produces reactive stimuli > process > manifestation of outcome = I realize she is off today.

The result of the rapid sequence of behaviours is that I realize I have to prepare some notes, followed by the thought, *I want to call the secretary to type the notes*, and then I remember that she is off today. Beyond a shadow of a doubt, it feels as if I am actively thinking about all this while in fact the brain pushes it to my awareness screen as it reaches the threshold of awareness (minimum requirements to enter the awareness screen) and is the outcome of complex brain processes.

While I am writing this, I am fully aware that I am writing because I am consciously selecting the words. In fact, these words that come to mind are produced by my brain process and pushed to my awareness screen. Just before this instant, I was not aware I was writing. I just wrote and consciously chose my words and corrected some sentences, or at least that is how it feels. Now I am consciously aware I am writing, and picking up my cup to sip some hot chocolate. I am aware that I hear voices and other sounds in the place where I sit. When you are talking with someone or watching a TV program you may know what you are talking about or what you are seeing on the TV, but you may not be consciously aware of being aware of it. This is often expressed when people say something like, "I am actually in a canoe and am going down the rapids," or, "I am playing in the finals, I am really playing for the championship." When canoeing down the rapids, you may be concentrating and working hard to keep the canoe from tipping over. You are in the moment and aware of the dangers around you and reacting to it. That does not mean that you are aware that you are aware of going down the rapids. That is a deeper level of awareness.

Here is another example. You may not be aware that your cell phone is ringing. You had your cell phone in your hand and laid it on a small table. After several minutes, you look for the phone but don't see it. Then someone close to you says, "It is lying on that little table where you put it." You look somewhat surprised and say, "I don't even remember putting it there." When you put the phone down you were not sleeping. You did not drop it beside the small table but placed it on top. You must have been aware of the table to place the cell phone there. By your own omission, you were not consciously aware of the act of putting down the cell phone. We may therefore say with some confidence that the brain continued to process stimuli and orchestrated you to put the cell phone exactly on the table where you put it. In that sense, the brain had processed stimuli (information) about the exact location of the table and coordinated movement for the cell phone to be put there. The point I am trying to make is that many decisions are being made or actions performed of which we are not consciously aware or which we do not consciously and deliberately construct.

Backtracking somewhat, remember that the instant we become aware of something, it may change due to new stimuli being processed. Becoming aware of something causes a new process, producing new outcomes that make us feel as if we are making the conscious decisions. It feels like this because we are not and cannot be consciously aware of the brain processes that produce outcomes, which we may manifest in behaviour as they meet the threshold of behaviour. Awareness also plays a role in the definition of *I* when I say, "I decided to stay home." At a deeper level, *I* is the self-realization of the brain through awareness; that *I* initiates the manifestation of the brain process through the statement: "I am staying home." In other words, the brain tells the brain to say, "I am staying home." Nevertheless, it feels as if I made the decision to stay home, regardless of what happens in the brain. It is manifested in a sentence that uses I, as in, "I go to work." Every time we say I, it is a manifestation of the *I* that is initiated by the brain, which represents itself as a self-realization through awareness: I. We are designed to function as we do with the feeling that causes us to believe we are in control and can do as we please. We would not feel this if we were not meant to feel this. That feeling gives us a sense of responsibility and accountability. The sense of responsibility and accountability are stimuli that are processed and contribute to the outcomes, thus impacting our behaviour in one way or another.

We may have wondered whether we are mere robots if we cannot do as we please. In response, I reply that awareness is the key factor influencing our behaviour. We need to feed ourselves with stimuli that produce—after being processed—the desired outcomes we believe we want. We want these because of brain processes. When we read, hear or experience something and these stimuli trigger our conscious awareness, then this awareness affects the brain processes that follow, as mentioned earlier. I also mentioned that we could look at awareness as a weighing factor. When various stimuli of similar nature trigger conscious awareness, they increase the likelihood that a certain kind of pathway will be developed in the brain. This means, in layman's terms, that the brain may start seeking certain stimuli, process them, and push the outcomes to our awareness screen. In other words, we become more often consciously aware of something. For example, we become consciously aware of our reaction to certain stress-producing events or circumstances, or of our angry response when a person does not agree with us.

From my personal experience, I can say that this book was the result of such a process. A simple question started a process that developed over thirty years. The first question triggered conscious awareness about the question. This stimulus was processed and produced outcomes. Those outcomes, upon appearing on my awareness screen, were instantly processed again as stimuli but now affected by the awareness factor. So, we could say that the process is self-generating, meaning stimuli is processed, causing the brain to seek more related stimuli (information), which in turn is processed together with other stimuli and these processes may produce thoughts we never had before. That is Procirclism in motion. This can become a routine process of the brain, manifested by an expression when I say, "I wonder why a person made that decision and whether people think about whether they could or could not have made a different choice." I could say that I have decided to pay attention to the behaviour of people and consciously decide to ask the question, "Why do we behave in a particular manner under specific circumstances?" Although understandable, saying this would be incorrect. The fact is that my brain is doing all the work and pushes outcomes to my awareness screen, and I experience it all in a very exciting way. At the same time, this process causes itself to dig even deeper into this subject.

A pressing question that may have been on your mind is, *Where is the control?* That is a very interesting question and is difficult to answer in a sentence. An alternate form of control may exist in the kind of stimuli our brain processes. The kind of stimuli being provided to the brain from all kinds of sources and being processed also has a big impact on the outcomes and thus our behaviour. When the brain is processing stimuli of a positive nature, the related outcomes will likely produce more positive behaviour. I realize this statement is simple and in real life it is much more complex, but the concept is the same.

During therapy sessions, we are provided with certain stimuli and it is anticipated that we will respond, over time, in a certain manner. That is, in fact, all that therapy attempts to do—provide information through many discussions or other means that will be beneficial to us and affect us positively. We may hear something like, "That is not your fault," or, "What you did for that person was very special," and that can have a positive impact on us. That was the result of process rather than mere choice. Medication does the same thing when it alters behaviour. Medication for bipolar, schizophrenia, and depression etc. alters behaviour because the medication affects parts of the brain so that it produces a scientifically anticipated outcome. We know that the same medication does not always produce the same results. This is because each brain is different and sometimes those differences prevent the medication from working as intended. Due to the complexity of the brain, we may not always know what causes medication not to work as intended. Reading this book will produce stimuli and triggers. The outcome for each is still to be determined. Reading certain parts again may prompt more questions and it may cause a thinking process never experienced before. It may alter some behaviour and it may increase our awareness as, stimulated by the content of this book, more stimuli may trigger conscious awareness which in turn will produce outcomes we manifest in behaviour.

We could say that awareness stops our automated brain processes for a moment and reprocesses it again after it has gone through our awareness screen and produces a different outcome. Our conscious awareness will have this effect. Reading this book will stimulate our conscious awareness. To what extent and over what period will be determined from person to person. If anything, we experience affects our behaviour and the choices we make, then we need to have a closer look at what we, in general, and our children, in particular, are exposed to. Again, not all stimuli affect every person in the same way.

In North America, we live in a capitalistic world. Wealth and power drive much of our behaviour. Perhaps we should ask at what cost. Products and services are sold only when there is demand for it. To earn money, companies need to sell their products and services. Thus, it creates a desire for the products and services offered. Advertisements are created to accomplish that. Guess why so much money is paid to advertise products and services? Without knowing it, companies are using the procirclistic model to achieve this. They feed us with information (commercials) for which they often have scientific evidence that these stimuli will influence a targeted group of potential customers to buy their products or services. These companies are not shooting from the hip and spending millions of dollars on advertising in the hope that it may work. Sometimes they can be wrong, but most often their advertisements work for a specific group of people. These people's behaviour must be, to a certain degree, predictable.

Remember when I said earlier that all behaviour is predictable but cannot be predicted? This is a classic example. These companies cannot predict all behaviour with 100% accuracy because there are too many factors (stimuli) unknown to them that are being processed by the brain. In addition, they do not— and likely could not —know all the stimuli that each brain processes, how these stimuli interact with each other, or how the individual brain functions to its smallest detail. This is the quality of each brain and this quality is dynamic, meaning it changes. However, if we could know the entire unknown to its smallest detail, I believe we could predict behaviour.

I have raised the question, What is I? It is quite possible that many have never asked this question or even thought about I in the way I have done in this book. Talking about it may bring it to the awareness of many people who have not thought about it before. Unless a sentence/stimulus like this triggers a process, we might not become aware of it. Even when the question is not asked directly, it may be the result of something else that is stimulated and causes a chain of thoughts, eventually leading to the question, What is I? That is what happened in my case. I had never heard anybody asking it, nor have I ever heard or read a statement that questions the existence of I or provided a definition of it that put everything in a different perspective. Yet, I started asking this question and I believe asking it is the result of a brain process that may have taken place over many years, for me to finally ask that question. Asking the question is not the result of choice but process. Part of that process is also that the brain produced many relevant factors of which I became aware when they were pushed onto my awareness screen and it produced insights in the decision-making process that are all part of this phenomenon. I describe it as the brain producing outcomes that in turn can stimulate a process that produces more relevant outcomes. It is what I experienced myself and it demonstrates how my concept developed and is the result of a process and not of trying to justify and explain a foregone conclusion or belief. In my opinion I cannot have a better and more reliable source than my own experience.

Awareness Under a Microscope

Before I am aware of a thought, I am not aware of that thought. When I want to think about something, I am already thinking about it. We must not compare thinking about something with physically searching for a file in a filing cabinet. Anytime we think about something it is already in our mind and we are aware of it. We cannot search for something we are not consciously aware of. In other words, we cannot try to think about something we are not yet thinking about. Anything we think about is the result of a brain process we are not aware of. A stimulus initiates a thought through a brain process and that thought is pushed to our awareness screen at which moment we then think about it (are aware of it). However, it feels as if we consciously bring up the thought or that we choose to think about it. This process, by which we become aware of our thoughts, may only take milliseconds. Because of the incredible speeds of these processes and the fact we are not consciously aware of it, it makes us feel as if we are truly thinking about what we want. It feels as if we are selecting the thought we want to have. The brain process is too fast for us to be consciously aware of and keep track of. So, even when we feel like we are choosing to think about something, it has already appeared, in one form or another, on our awareness screen, and then we think about it. If it had not appeared on our awareness screen we would not have been able to think about it and we would not be able to think, that we did not think about it. What we are not aware of, we cannot think about. In a way it is funny when we say that we are not thinking about the accident that happened yesterday while saying this demonstrates that we do.

Awareness is a key element in our brain processes and plays a significant role in the kind of outcomes produced. Because of the significance of awareness, I keep returning to some of the information I have provided earlier but approach it from different angles. Thoughts are continuously supplied and when they meet the threshold of awareness, we become aware of them. That is when we say, "I am thinking about it," or when we are just thinking about something. I do not bring the thoughts up or supply them. Remember what we discussed about I in a previous chapter? Unless I is an independently functioning entity and can be identified as such, it cannot supply thoughts. The definition of *I* excludes it from any form of independency or being an entity that operates independently of the brain. When we become aware of thoughts, they are instantly processed as stimuli at lightning fast speeds, and new outcomes are produced. They may cause new thoughts and the cycle repeats itself. To us it feels as if we are thinking and bringing up these thoughts ourselves. I cannot argue with that feeling. This feeling is supported by the fact that we are not aware of the brain processes that take place which means to us that those processes may as well not be happening. Thus, as each brain process produces outcomes, the outcomes also affect the next brain process. The latter is important and makes the whole process dynamic, thus even more complex. When we are being reminded to be polite, the message is being processed and produces an outcome. In this example, being polite is a stimulus. The process, in which among other stimuli, being polite is also processed, leaves something behind and affects the next process. If the stimulus, being polite, was not part of this process, then the next process of the brain would produce a different outcome, even if all other stimuli were the same.

After the stimulus (being polite) is processed as a stimulus, it may trigger greater awareness of being polite, which the brain itself is generating through the impact of awareness on that stimulus. Now, new thoughts may pop up in our mind, triggered by that being-polite stimulus through our awareness. The brain may assemble related thoughts and push them to our awareness screen, which may cause a greater impact on the assemblage of new thoughts that are related. This may trigger cycles that can be called brain pathways. From my personal experience, one question set such a cycle in motion, which then grew stronger as the brain assembled more and more related thoughts that in return fueled the process to an even greater extent.

The essence of awareness is much deeper than our general understanding of being aware of something. Awareness lies at the core of our humanity. To get a grasp of its depth we can follow a procession from *I am aware of it* to *I am consciously aware of it* and still deeper yet, to *I am aware that I am aware*. Eventually, we reach a plateau where words fail to describe the depth of awareness that may briefly appear to us, somehow, somewhere. Everything which we become consciously aware of is instantly affected by that awareness, which is immediately being processed as an additional stimulus, causing an outcome that is different than the previous one. This can be manifested by saying something like, "I have changed my mind." It feels as if the moment we realize something, we think quickly and come up with a different thought or double down on the existing one. Either result is produced from the additional awareness stimulus in combination with a host of other stimuli.

Our awareness is continuously being supplied with thoughts. Yes, I am saying "being supplied." I don't provide these thoughts nor can I. Remember if we suggest that I do supply them then we go back to the issue about *I*. In that case, the following question requires an answer suggesting that *I* is an independent entity that by itself can direct the brain towards what to do. Here is that question: What is *I*, that it could supply thoughts? Yes, I mean exactly what I wrote. It is not an error. It must be read as this: What is the vehicle that supplies our thoughts? Thoughts supplied to our awareness and which we become consciously aware of, cause stimuli to be processed by the brain. Without knowing what has happened, we experience another thought that may feel as if we have changed our mind.

The quality of the stimuli is a contributing factor in the determination of the outcome when the brain processes it. When we read, when we hear something, when we get advice, these are all stimuli and are processed by the brain. These processes produce outcomes but they also affect the next brain process. I have discussed this in an earlier chapter and would like to return briefly to the *being polite* factor. When the message of being polite is given and received, it is processed and produces outcomes. It also leaves something—we could say it a residue—behind, and that affects the next process. So the next stimuli, to a certain extent, when processed, are or may also be affected by the message of being polite. The internal brain processes determine if and how the next processes are affected by it. The outcome of these processes may trigger greater awareness of being polite, and new thoughts produced in the brain will be supplied to our awareness. Slowly but gradually, in this case, politeness is becoming a subject of importance to us. It did not happen by choice although it surely feels like it; it happens by process. Something like this happened to me as I described earlier. One question set a process in motion and it has not ended yet. I am frequently aware of procirclistic events when I watch how people describe the choices they make or why they changed their mind. No matter how we turn or twist it, our feeling about it does not change. We strongly feel that we are making our choices freely and if we wanted to, could simply make a different choice, even though we do not.

Every time we change our mind, we truly believe that we just thought about it and decided to do it differently. We show it by saying, "I had to think about it for a minute but changed my mind." We are unaware of the brain process that produced an outcome which we manifested when we changed our choice. When we become consciously aware of something, it may activate our sense of morality, sensitivity, our ethical values or our beliefs. This happens in our brain by means of a complex process in which transmission of chemicals that the brain produces may be included. Perhaps we can recall moments when our immediate reaction to a question was yes, and a little later changed to no. I am sure many people have experienced this when it came to the question: Are you for capital punishment? They may have said yes, but after thinking about it for a moment, many might have changed it to no. Put differently, certain stimuli activate other factors or values. When we become consciously aware of outcomes being pushed to our awareness screen, they are intensified (weighing factor). When processed as a stimulus, together with a host of other stimuli, they may activate a multitude of different elements, which ethical and moral values may be a part of, among many others. The weighing factor relates to weight of a stimulus, meaning that it has a bigger (high-weighing factor) or lesser impact (low-weighing factor). Anything that appears on our awareness screen and we become consciously aware of instantly has a high-weighing factor simply because we become consciously aware of it. When we say, "I changed my mind," it is already changed, and that change is pushed to our awareness screen and expressed as, "I changed my mind." Although it is an illusion, it certainly feels as if we are consciously changing our mind at will. We even thought about factors that we considered before changing our mind. Yet, it was all pushed to our awareness because of brain processes. Awareness (as the awareness factor) can trigger a host of brain processes, that in combination with other stimuli produce a different outcome than the previous one and when manifested it causes us to say, "I changed my mind," or, "I made up my mind." In fact, the brain moves into a certain direction as stimulation creates more stimulation and in turn that creates more stimulation—the weighing factor of awareness.

There is no argument with feeling as if we are making the choices we please, but it does not mean that we may comfortably build our thesis upon it. If we do, then we must be able to answer some of the most challenging questions about beliefs we hold on to simply for no other reason than that they are assumed to be true.

We have discussed many of them earlier and include questions such as, what is I? and why do we ask for motives and reasons for our actions? If we believe that we can make any choices at any time under any circumstances (with the understanding that they normally would allow other choices to be made) as we please, why do we need therapists or psychologists, and why is psychology being taught? It is quite evident that our behaviours do not support a belief that suggests we can do whatever we want whenever we want, or could easily have done something different than what we did. Procirclism seems to support our behaviours and justifies our search for reasons, motives and factors that contribute to them. It supports the study of psychology, psychiatry, neuroscience and teachings of good parenting skills. I could continue for quite some time with real life evidence of support for the theory of Procirclism. However, the strongest opposition is that we don't feel that we cannot do as we please. I believe in court that would be a very weak argument, when countered with real life behavioural examples proving the opposite.

Procirclism describes the importance of what kind of stimuli is feeding our brain. When we listen to positive, constructive information that may stimulate an increased attention to positive and constructive information, we say, "I have decided to listen to more positive and constructive information." In fact, the external stimuli, when being processed, produce outcomes that activate a greater interest in positive and constructive information. For this reason, conscious awareness is important. We know that bullying has pushed some people to suicidal behaviour. This does not mean that everybody who is being bullied becomes suicidal. However, that can under no circumstance diminish the harmful potential of bullying. Just as the harmful content of certain products can under no circumstance be diminished because they may not have harmed most people. The irony is that poisonous materials must be stored in places where children cannot have access to them and because poisonous materials can cause various degrees of injuries, safety rules have been put into place. Yet, when it comes to psychological harm, we still refuse to apply the same safety precautions. I understand that the risk of injury when using poisonous materials is much greater than the risk of injury when being exposed to harmful psychological material. Having said this, the question is, What drives our actions? Are our actions driven by money, concern for safety, or other factors? If it is money, it is a stimulus used in the brain process and produces a different outcome than when the stimulus is a concern for safety. Neither money nor a concern for safety is the result of choice but it is the result of complicated brain processes that can result in money becoming a strong stimulus. Yet, it feels to us as if it is our choice to love money and make it the main motivator of our business decisions.

Thoughts

I have tried to consciously bring up thoughts and wonder where thoughts originate. How do they suddenly pop up in my mind? Can I consciously bring up any thoughts that I want? I find from my own experience that I do not consciously think about having a certain thought in my mind. Before I become aware of the thought, I am not aware of it. If I am already aware of a thought, I don't have to bring it up anymore because it is already there. So how does it pop up in my mind? If it does not seem possible for me to think about a thought before it is in my mind, how does it get there? It is part of the procirclistic process, or what I would call, the procirclistic brain process, where a thought is produced and pushed to our awareness screen because of a complex operation where stimuli are being processed and produce outcomes. When these outcomes pass the manifestation threshold, they are manifested in behaviour. While I write this, I am becoming consciously aware of this question. As such, I realize it has become a stimulus that puts a process in motion that produces outcomes I can experience as thoughts. I repeat myself when I say that it feels as if I brought this thought up at will. I realize that no willful effort is required to bring up thoughts, in fact, no willful force can ever bring up any thoughts. Thoughts appear as they do and it is impossible to want to think about a thought without knowing what thought. When I know what thought I want to think about, I have already been aware of it; I am already thinking about it. This makes me realize that our brain processes happen in such rapid succession and that our awareness is always behind, even if it is only a millisecond or less, giving the illusion that we think about something because we want to think about it. Even when it feels like this to us, it does not mean that this is what is happening.

The reverse is true. First comes the process that produces an outcome, which can be a thought. When the thought appears on our awareness screen, we feel that the thought appeared because we wanted it. In fact, we want to think about it, because it was produced as an outcome. Since we cannot willfully bring up thoughts because we cannot think about them before we are thinking about them, this means we can only want to think about something that has already been produced as an outcome by a brain process. Sometimes we say that we did not want to think about it but nevertheless the thought did appear. It demonstrates that our will had no power over the thought. It just appeared as it did. We know it did not just appear but was caused or produced by a process of various stimuli. Because we are not consciously aware of these processes, it can and does feel as if thoughts appear as we want them to appear. I cannot argue with that feeling because it is a true feeling and is, as strange as it may sound, produced by the absence of our awareness regarding any brain processes that produce outcomes, causing us to feel we can do as we please/want.

Memories

Reading this can provide a stimulus to the brain that brings up a memory. Only because we are not aware of the brain process that produces a memory, can it feel to us as if we are in control of memories that appear in our mind. When we say we are trying to remember something, we are not remembering it yet, but when we specify what we want to remember, then we are already remembering it. It's the same with our thoughts. The process that applies to the production of our thoughts also applies to memories. We cannot recall a memory we are not aware of yet, and subsequently we cannot consciously choose what memories we want to bring up. A complex process causes memories to pop up in our mind. Just as with our thoughts, when a memory pops up, it feels as if we wanted to bring it while in fact, when we experience the memory, it is because it is already produced. If we say, "I want to remember that," it is the memory that is already there and for that reason we want to remember it. No conscious willful effort on our part has anything to do with what individual memories we become aware of. That may not reflect what we feel is happening when we remember something, but that is how it is. It is impossible to want to remember a specific memory before we have it. If we know what we want to remember, we are already remembering it, right? As soon as we become aware of a memory, it is instantly processed and produces another outcome, which may be in the form of a different memory. That new memory is stimulated by the previous memory through awareness and the result of a new process.

The decision-making processes our brains perform are complex. No matter how the choices we make are determined, it feels as if we are making them, or are at least able to make them. That also relates to choosing the memories we want to consciously remember. Because it feels so real, most people believe that we can choose/do anything we want. Most of us also believe that we could have chosen a different memory, thought, action or behaviour other than the one we did, if we simply wanted to do this. That belief is founded in our experienced feelings, but it does not mean that it also happens like that. When we have a fever, we may experience real coldness while in fact we are warm. Here our experience (feeling) is different from our actual body temperature. In another instance we may feel as if another person has been rude to us while in fact, after we have received more information, it was not the case at all. Does that mean our feeling was wrong? No, not at all because it is what we truly felt. We can all recall feelings we had, and later discovered that those feelings were not representative of what happened. Perception may also have something to do with this, besides a multitude of stimuli that are processed by the brain in an extremely complex manner that includes the inner workings of our brain, and chemicals produced and used in any brain processes. When I talk about brain processes, it is all-inclusive, meaning that factors yet unknown to us may also be involved, which we will discover later.

CHAPTER 6

PERCEPTION

How often have we heard someone say something like, "I did not perceive it that way," or, "If I could perceive it the way you do, then I would see that your reaction makes sense." If it meets the threshold of manifestation, perception plays a significant role in the brain processes of information (stimuli) to produce outcomes that we manifest in behaviours. Yet we rarely think about our perceptions and whether they should be different to have a better or more accurate understanding of information provided to us. Perception is always present. We can look at it as the personalization of information we receive. Information (stimuli) is personalized when it filters through our perception—the perception factor. Generally, we are not consciously aware of the impact of the perception factor. Our experiences are what we experience and are already affected by the perception factor when we have them. It is not that we experience something, and are then aware it changes; it is being filtered by the perception factor. Perception begins to develop with the first brain process that takes place and it is dynamic. It changes and causes us not to perceive similar information (data/stimuli) in the same manner. Sometimes that difference may hardly be noticeable while at other times it seems quite obvious. At times, information of a kind may upset us while at other times it does not. I have heard people say, "Since you told me this, I understand what I heard before was completely different and makes me angry." The information I just heard shines a different light on the information I had before and to which, at that time, I did not react with anger. Now, with the additional information, I perceive the previous information differently and it makes me angry. It shows that perception is not static and is easily affected by other stimuli (information).

We must recognize that two different stimuli, when processed, produce different outcomes from when one stimulus affects the other stimulus, resulting in a different perspective and outcome. That different perspective is the result of one stimulus affecting another stimulus, which is then perceived differently and processed as a different stimulus, producing a different outcome. For instance, we hear that one person badly beat another person. Our first reaction is that we are angry with the person who did the beating. We perceive it as a senseless attack. After we hear that the person who was beaten tried to rape a young girl, our anger towards the person who did the beating subsides and now leans toward the person who attempted to rape. The perception of the beating has changed because of additional information we received. Perception, rather than anything else, played a significant role in the change of the outcome as the beating was viewed differently. Now we do not perceive the beating as a senseless assault anymore but as an attempt to protect a victim. Our first perception was later affected by additional information (stimuli).

Perception plays a big role but is not always recognized by us as a factor that taints how we perceive something. The logic behind this is simple. We can only experience what we experience in the way we experience it. If something makes us angry, it is a fact, but it feels as if the information caused our anger. We are not thinking that our perception has affected the essence of the information in a way that now makes us angry. We would not have become angry if our perception was different. However, when we bring the awareness factor into play, it triggers awareness of our mood and plays a role in how we perceive the information. If this happens, it is also part of another brain process and may produce an outcome that is void of anger when manifested in behaviour. One may find similarity with some stoic principles, which judgement are left for the reader to make.

All data or stimuli that is processed goes through the interpretation factor, which affects, in various degrees, how information or data is being seen or experienced. For instance, driving on a rural road with a maximum speed limit of 50 km/h, we are suddenly passed by a speeding car. It startles us and some of us may put our middle finger up or mumble some unkind words. Such reactions are often based on the belief or interpretation that the driver of the speeding car is reckless, has no consideration for other drivers or is perhaps showing off. Later, by accident, we discover that this driver had an emergency. His wife was involved in a serious car accident and rushed to the hospital in critical condition. This new information will shed a different perspective on the speeding driver and suddenly our anger makes way for compassion. The information did not change but the perception did. This whole process leaves something behind in our brain. If a similar situation happens again, instead of immediately getting angry or make a rude gesture, we may suddenly consider that extreme speeding may be due to an emergency. In this case, a different perspective affects the event, and the brain process produces a different outcome, which we manifest in behaviour.

Perception happens and is the result of brain processes in whatever way, shape or form they take place. It is a fact that people do not perceive everything in the same way. How often do we say that we have a different perception? A different perception can affect stimuli in a big way and body language can also be perceived differently. Depending on personal experiences, one person may perceive a friendly, open and polite person as trustworthy, while another becomes very suspicious of them.

The processes in our brain are complex. Perception, for instance, influences our emotions, thus impacting the outcome of a process and our behaviour. The reverse is also true. Emotions influence perception and, as such, the outcome of a process and our behaviour. In brain processes, interactions among the various stimuli take place. None of us consciously regulates perception and emotions, but when we become consciously aware of a perception or emotion, the awareness factor plays a role and results in stimuli that impacts perception or emotion, resulting in a different outcome. Our emotions and perceptions happen on a regular basis and we may say that they are triggered. When pushed to our awareness as outcomes, an immediate process takes place again because the awareness factor becomes an additional factor.

Perception and Outcomes

One can easily understand that our brain is complex, though we can't comprehend its processes easily. There is the full spectrum of all stimuli that are being processed, how they interact with each other at lightning-fast speeds, and how each process and its outcomes affect the next process. If stimuli were processed without the effects of the previous process and its outcome, how could that outcome not be different than with the effect of the previous process and its outcome? One may wonder whether we will ever be able to observe all the stimuli and their interactions during brain processes. This means being able to observe the full working of our brain in its finest detail. In the meantime, new discoveries may be made, presently still unknown to us.

We have seen that so many factors play a role in the decision-making process that it is getting more and more difficult to defend the belief that behaviour is simply a matter of independent choice and free of any influence, rather than it being the result of process. When we need to find the answer to a math problem, we will not pick any number and determine that this number is the answer that solves the problem. For instance, when we add 4 and 4, then subtract 1 and multiply this by 5, we do not say the answer is 18. The outcome of the math problem is hidden in the process of the elements of the math problem. In other words, it is hidden in the outcome of a process, not a random process. We add 4 and 4 and the outcome is 8. Eight is the result of a process that adds 4 plus 4. Now we need to subtract 1 and the outcome is 7. Again, this is not a random number but the outcome of another process that subtracts 1 from 8. At last we need to multiply 7 by 5 and the outcome is 35. We see that 35 is not just a random number we picked, but it is the result of a process that multiplied 7 by 5 and produced 35 as the only possible outcome. In a similar way, our brain processes stimuli that produce outcomes that we manifest in our behaviour. As the outcomes of math problems are the result of processing numbers, so is our behaviour the result of processing stimuli. In math, perception plays no role nor does emotion because it is impossible to change the correct outcome of 2 + 2. It is always the same. Neither outcome is the result of choice. Math contains many formulas, sometimes at a more advanced and complex stage, but remains straightforward. Brain processes can be extremely complex. We can visually observe the math process. When I say we cannot observe our brain processes, I mean that none of us feel that our brain is processing stimuli and produces outcomes. With math, we can make connections between the process and the outcomes. With brain processes we cannot make the same connections, as we are not consciously aware of the processes.

When specific information (stimuli) is pushed to our awareness screen we become aware of them as factors (information) that contribute to our choices (we are making the connection between specific influences and our choices). Sometimes this information affects our perception, thus affecting the outcome of the brain process. In this case, we can make the connection between influences that change our perception (how we see something). In addition, we may become aware that a different perception contributes to a different outcome, thus behaviour. Nevertheless, it feels to us as if we are consciously doing as we please. Translating this into mathematical terms would be like saying that we could choose the outcome of 2 + 2 from any number we know of. In math, this is impossible because there is only one correct answer.

Perception is often a strong contributor to the way we see, experience and feel things. We do not consciously control our perception. Perception is continuously influenced by many other factors and is therefore not static. Emotions also contribute very strongly to the way we sense, experience and perceive things. Both emotions and perceptions affect outcomes of brain processes and thus our behaviour. Both change frequently because they are consistently influenced by many other factors.

CHAPTER 7

WILL

When reading this chapter, you may feel that I am making repetitive statements, and to an extent you are right. The reason for this is that I am writing this book in the form of Procirclism. In the procirclistic model, many aspects are processed by the brain as stimuli and produce outcomes. Aspects of stimuli may be processed repeatedly after they produce outcomes that are pushed to our awareness screen and then reprocessed. My repetitive statements and issues resemble the process of Procirclism and offer different perspectives. On the other hand, I feel it does not hurt to be repetitive in the sense of a reminder of the complexity and originality of Procirclism, because what is repeated is key to this concept.

When I use the word "will," it is important to define its meaning. When I say, "I want to do this," it does not mean that I am actually doing it. It is a desire. I like or prefer to do it. Depending on many factors, I may or may not do it. In the simple sentence, "I want to do this," we must focus on I and want. Questions like *What is I?* and *What is making the decisions?* Are of paramount importance, but most of us have never asked these questions. Yet life continues without any earthshaking events, even though we did not ask these questions. Because of its importance, I have discussed the *I phenomenon* in a previous chapter. Once again, we will have a closer look at I. When I reread the previous sentences, I put my hands underneath my chin and look at the computer screen. Suddenly, I realize I am putting my hands underneath my chin. Thinking out loud, I realize I did not consciously want to do this, nor did I not want to do it; I just did it. I know that I could have done something different, like folded my arms. Now I become consciously aware and look at my arms while I am folding them in front of my chest, but I don't feel a strenuous effort on my part that forces my arms to fold. I am asking myself whether I could not have folded my arms at the instant I did fold them. I know I could have put them up or let them hang down, but I didn't. I know that a variety of other actions could have been performed, but the fact is, I did not perform any of them but only the one.

I look around the café and observe a lot of actions taking place. A woman lifts her cup to her mouth and sips while reading a paper. At the same time, a man is taking his sandwich out of the paper it is wrapped in. I wonder whether they could have done anything else. I assume the woman was not consciously thinking about every detail of her actions that resulted in a cup going up and reaching her mouth while her eyes followed the text of the paper she was reading. Whether the action was either deliberately or consciously made, it was nevertheless made. I realized that all our actions, whether verbally or physically expressed, are not a matter of choice but are the result of processes. They happen the way they do because of an uncountable number of other factors that play a role in the processes. They do not happen as they do without the impact of contributing factors. The complex process of all known and unknown factors is influenced by the brain process itself and determines outcomes that we manifest in behaviour. Knowledge of actions other than those we express in behaviour is just that— knowledge. They are not options from which we can choose if we want to because the circumstances are the same and the same contributing factors are being processed by the same brain process and produce the same outcomes. Doing the same thing, we will get the same result, if everything is precisely the same, 2 + 2 = 4. You want 5? You must change something in the equation to get 5. No matter how many other actions we know and which can be performed, in the end, we can only manifest one; we are only able to perform one action at a time. In fact, what we believe to be other options that we can choose if we want to, are not. That is just knowledge of other actions we can perform. That is different from being able to choose other options. We refer to options as other choices we can make, as we please, because that is how it feels to us, but even when it feels like that it does not mean that it is that way. Our actions are our actions just as the action of a car is that it moves along on a road or of a boat gliding over water. The car can roll over and the boat can capsize, yet they rarely do. A car does not simply roll over or a boat capsize. If they do, there are reasons and those reasons are different from those that keep the car moving along the road or the boat gliding over the water. If there were no other different factors (reasons/stimuli) present for the car to roll over and the boat to capsize, we could never feel safe in a car or boat. It is the same with our behaviour. We would never feel safe again if someone could harm others based on the same factors that produce non-harmful behaviour. In other words, there would be no reasons for any kind of behaviour we exhibit. We could do what we want but have no clue as to why we want what we want. In that case, no one should ever question our behaviour? The answer is one of silence because we would not understand that question nor would anyone ever ask it.

There are many actions that cannot be performed at the same time. Furthermore, we cannot act and not act at the same time. For instance, we can be talking and walking but not walking and running or walking and sitting. When we talk, we cannot be quiet. When we move our fingers, we cannot move them forward and backward at the same time. We are never consciously orchestrating every single motion or action we perform. Many of them just happen but not randomly. They are all the result of brain processes but it does not feel that way. So, where does will fit in? Before we do anything, we may have wanted to do it. The meaning of that will is desire. What we want to do is the result of brain processes. Now, it is still just a desire, orchestrated by a brain process. Sometimes we recognize the contributing factors, for example when we want to go on vacation to Florida because the weather is warmer there and it is winter where we live. When we decide to buy US dollars today because we anticipate the US dollar becoming more expensive in days to come. A great number of contributing factors remain unrecognized. These are two simple examples where we recognize some factors that contribute to the choices we make. Often it is more complex and we do not recognize all the contributing—if not determining—factors to the choices we make.

We can also approach will from a completely different perspective when we look at will as a force of doing something. We do it because we want (will) to do it. In this case, it is not a preference. Will, in that sense, is the force necessary to manifest behaviour. When we exercise this will—meaning how we behave—it is a force that is produced by a brain process and embedded in the outcome. Thus for example, when the outcome of a brain process is traveling to New York, then embedded in that outcome is a force called will. Such a will is directly linked to the outcomes; it is not subject to choice. Will then, does not direct something to go in one direction or another. Will is the force that manifests behaviour as it appears. In that sense, will is not free, neither is it free. When we say that we have free will we are making will a subject as if will is an independent entity that can decide what it wants, as in being free. Will as the force necessary to manifest behaviour, cannot be qualified as an independent entity that can choose, because will is embedded in each outcome, not as freedom to choose, but as a force to manifest. Questions such as whether the will can be free dissipate and make no sense. Only in our imagination does will, as free will or not free will, become an issue.

Complex brain processes produce outcomes that are manifested in behaviour. Awareness plays a major role in these processes and outcomes, and thus the behaviour we manifest. Will is produced. We do not choose what we will although to most of us it feels that we do. What we do, we want to do. In other words, we will it. In that sense, we cannot will anything else other than that what we do. We do it, and therefore we will it. This may seem backwards, but this is to illustrate that will is embedded in the outcomes and does not exist outside of it as an independent entity.

What we will is the result of a process, not a choice. At the instant an action is performed, there is no choice involved. The brain process produces only outcomes and no options from which I can choose. Remember, there is no independent entity called *I* that forces our brain to function in such a manner that it performs an action that *I* desires. Here we must read *I*, in the sense of it being something and not in the sense of it being a pronoun. Knowing that different actions can be performed has convinced us that we could have performed them at the time we performed a different action. When we perform an action (behaviour) and later say, "I was not aware I did that," it does not indicate that we consciously scanned other actions that could have been performed. We did what we did without consciously being aware of it.

It is impossible for us to experience brain processes and sense an outcome as the only outcome and only behaviour we can manifest. No one can feel or describe what the brain does when it is working and processing stimuli. In neuroscience instruments are being used to show brain activity but the person is unaware of what is happening in his brain. What we believe to be other possible choices we could have made but did not are illusive choices that could not have been made unless something else in the process was different.

The question we have asked for centuries has steered us in the wrong direction. There is no answer unless we force one that cannot be defended to the end. That question is whether we have free will or not. This question can never be answered. You may think it can because almost everyone has a belief about it. That belief is that we do have free will. However, we do not have free will nor do we not have free will. There is just will, the force necessary to manifest behaviour that constitutes seamless behaviour.

Knowing that options other than the ones we manifest are performable is just that, knowledge. That knowledge must not be confused with believing that any of the other performable behaviours could have been manifested without anything else having been different.

I am aware of my typing at this moment and stop for a second before pressing the next key. I see all the keys in front of me. I push one key but can also see all the other ones I did not push. I was aware of them but not in the sense I could have pushed any of them. That is because the key I pushed is the one I wanted to, otherwise I would not have pushed it. My will to push that key is the result of the process of stimuli that produced an outcome which I manifested by pushing that key. If I change my mind and move my finger to another key and push that one, it is the result of another brain process producing a different outcome that I manifested in a different action executed by my will and the only will that prompted me to push a different key. In both examples, the first key I pressed followed by a change of mind when I pressed a different one are the result of process and not choice.

Will cannot be qualified by being free or not. We would never ask whether it can also be correct for 8 + 8 to be a different number than 16. We don't ask because we know it is the only outcome; 8 + 8 cannot have two different but correct answers. When it comes to the choices we make, we say that there are many options to choose from. Sometimes we experience making a choice as being extremely difficult. You see, it feels as if we consciously make choices. When asked when and where we want to go on a vacation, there seems to be many options. Yet we pick one specific date, destination and duration. Could we have chosen any of the other so-called possibilities? If we talk about odds, for example, and have other people predicting the choices we would eventually make, the odds that they would predict correctly could be as high as 1:1000 if there were 1000 options available. So, to pick the choice we would make is often, if not always, against all odds. When applying the process as the basis for the choices we make rather than random free will, then it becomes clear that there are no choices, just outcomes we manifest in behaviour. It is that simple.

We can only will what the outcome produced and we subsequently will manifest in behaviour because will is embedded in the outcome. Will is not an external entity that directs the outcome. If will could direct the outcome it would mean that the answer to 2 + 2 is directed by an outside force that could come up with any number. The answer to 2 + 2 is embedded in 2 + 2, and in the same way, will is embedded in the outcome of a brain process. When we cannot speak of will in the sense of whether we have free will or not, we must define it to understand its purpose: Will is the force necessary to manifest behaviour. As such, in the outcome of brain processes lies a force that is will. It is necessary to manifest behaviour. Without force (will) behaviour cannot be manifested. That force can exist in our subconscious. It is embedded in the outcome and is not an independent entity. It is embedded as weight is embedded in objects. We cannot choose the weight of an object because the object owns the weight. Will as a force is also embedded in the outcomes of brain processes and as such we cannot qualify it as being free or not free; it simply is.

Free Will Debate

The free will debate is an illusory debate. When we ask whether we have free will, we expect to receive an answer. We have pondered this thought for centuries and are unable to agree. It is an intellectual debate that is clouded by what we feel to be real and what we are not consciously aware of: brain processes. Yet, as demonstrated before, we debate the free will issue and at the same time, strongly suggest that there are reasons for the decisions we make. Random free will that stands alone and is void of any influences is impossible to prove. The fact that in every aspect of our lives we consistently demonstrate that motives, illnesses, stress, fear or any other form of contributing factors play a role in our behaviour, provides a strong argument for the non-existence of an independent, random free will that stands alone and is void of any influences. Arguing that we do have free will makes it equally difficult or impossible because we demonstrate daily that we assume there are always reasons for what we do or do not do. We try to change people's minds by providing information which we believe may influence them. When we do not understand why certain actions are performed, we ask why (for example, this is why murder investigations always attempt to identify a motive). When we assume we have free will, it suggests that will is an independent entity that decides and orchestrates the brain to be in a condition to perform the action we have chosen. Certain activities take place in the brain to perform specific actions. These must be orchestrated by will because will, in its freedom, has chosen a specific behaviour. That is what free will means. When we define will as the force necessary to manifest behaviour and is embedded in brain processes, the question whether will is free or not is an impossible one. Will has the nature of the process by which it is produced as an apple is the fruit of an apple tree. No one expects an orange to grow on an apple tree.

Brain processes of stimuli produce will as a force. Its DNA is the stimuli that are being processed and the outcome they produce. In other words, when vacation time comes around and we must decide where we want to go, the brain processes stimuli and produces an outcome, which we manifest in behaviour. In that outcome is a force (will) to manifest the outcome. That force (will) will not have us run to the neighbor's and ask for some salt when we are trying to decide on a vacation. Yes, that sounds ridiculous, but the point I am making is that the nature of the stimuli being processed is embedded in the will it produces in the outcome. The force of will is not constant but dynamic. Not every process produces, in its outcome, the same strength of the will or force necessary to manifest the outcome in behaviour. If the will or force is too weak and does not meet the threshold of manifestation, there will be no manifestation of that outcome. For example, when deciding on a vacation, Russia comes briefly to mind but never comes up again. Deciding to vacation in Russia is not happening, and thus is not manifested in our behaviour. That does not mean that there is a void in our behaviour because manifested actions are void of that which is not manifested, and behaviour is therefore a continuous stream of manifested actions only. The brain works seamlessly and the outcomes of brain processes, manifested in our actions, are always perfect. They are perfect for no other reason than the fact that they are outcomes, and they are the only possible outcomes following the process of stimuli by which they are produced.

Whether we look at will as something we want, as in something we prefer or desire, or as in it is the power necessary to manifest behaviour, in both instances it is the result of a process to which freedom does not apply. It is produced by the process it is embedded in and therefore innate to the nature of the outcome of the process. When we look at will as in *I want to do that*, or *I prefer to do that*, will or desire does not exist until it is produced by a process of stimuli and is embedded in its outcome, manifested as *I want to do that*. Whether I will do it or not is not important and is irrelevant at that point.

What we will is ultimately to manifest the outcome of brain processes in behaviour. That is what we will because it is the outcome and the only outcome of the process of stimuli. When we talk about other possible behaviour we could have manifested but did not, we are speaking about illusory options. Moreover, what we see and accept as other possible choices are illusory choices that could not have been made unless something else in the process was different. The question we have asked for centuries has been the wrong question. It has set us on a path where we have found no answer.

Do we have free will? This is a misleading question and one that should never be asked because it cannot be answered. I must repeat myself, we do not have free will nor do we not have free will. There is just will, one at a time, and many in succession that constitutes seamless behaviour. Knowing that other actions can be performed is just that, knowing that other actions can be performed. But this must not be confused with a belief that we could have chosen a different action if we had wanted to. Therefore, regarding confusion, I mean that what we believe is not what also happens.

We believe we can do whatever we want while in fact, we cannot. If I dig a little deeper into this sentence I can say that we can do what we want because we always want what the process produces as an outcome. So, in fact, we always do what we want, but what we want is not the result of choice but of process.

When we know that other actions can be performed, it does not mean that they can be performed at any given time. All actions, before being performed, require a brain process to produce an outcome that is manifested in behaviour (action). Any action can only be manifested when it is the outcome of a brain process. For a different action to be manifested, something else must happen. We can see this illustrated in the earlier example of 2 + 2 = 4 and never another number. Will is always embedded in the outcome of the process of stimuli as the answer to a math problem is always embedded in the problem. The correct answer to a math problem is always the only one possible and the will of a brain process is always the only one possible to manifest the outcome of the brain process. Our will cannot be considered free or not.

As mentioned in the previous pages, I am aware of my typing at this moment regarding what keys I have pressed, am going to press or not press. I realize that I simply cannot perform a different action than the one I do, not because I don't have free will, but because my will is embedded in the outcome of brain processes resulting in the willing to do exactly what I do. I continue to believe that I could have willed something else because I feel that I am doing what I want to do and am ignorant of the process that produces that will. We will most likely never get away from the feeling that we always have different options we can choose from when faced with having to make a choice. Remember when discussing when and where we would go on a vacation. We pick one specific date, destination and duration. Could we have chosen any of the other possibilities? When applying the process as the basis for our choice rather than random free will, then there is only one choice at a time we can make. That does not mean that our choice is easier to predict because we do not know all the stimuli that contribute to the process or the part of the brain that is doing the processing. To predict the outcome (behaviour), everything contributing to the process must be known. In this example, we could only make (will) the choice we made, but many choices were known. The process produces one outcome, which we manifest in our behaviour. Yet we feel that we chose as we pleased. We did not choose any of the other options we knew. We willed to go on that date and to that destination for that period. This is where the definition of will plays a role. Will, as the force necessary to manifest behaviour, lies in the outcome of brain processes.

When I started writing this book, I did not know I would come to the conclusion that I came to. The process has taken me here. I witnessed my brain in action. Spontaneous thoughts popped into my mind, unrelated to the action I was involved in. I experienced, at a more conscious level, Procirclism, while I was writing about it. It developed along its own path, unrelated to any desired outcome I had at the outset. I just pondered the question of whether we have free will, which was inspired by a friend asking whether I thought I had free will.

I am convinced, for the first time, that the question of whether we have free will leads us along a path without an answer.

I would like to give one more illustration of how we can look at will where choice has no foothold. Just imagine for a moment that I have asked you and a few other people to only give the correct answer, as you see it. I will ask you to state the color you see in a glass, when I ask you, and not before. I take the glass and pour a little water in it. I then add three different colors of liquid. Now I ask you to tell me what color you see. You say blue and another person says green, and perhaps one person says yellow. Remember you can only say the truth as you see it. You saw that I mixed the water with three different colors of liquid. You knew that there were many colors but were not allowed to mention any of them, because I had asked you to say only the color you saw, and only when I asked. You were also only able to say the truth as you saw it at that time. Thus, the color that you and each of the other people mentioned is the color you and they saw, regardless what the color in the glass really was.

Let's go back to will. I have stated that will is the force necessary to manifest behaviour and that will is embedded in the outcome of the process. The color you mentioned, when I asked, is the only color you mention because you could only say the truth as you saw it. The will to manifest behaviour is the only behaviour you will manifest because it is the only outcome of the brain process. Just as the color you saw is the only color that was produced by mixing water with three different colors of liquid. That people saw different colors at the end is because of individualized perceptions. Just as perception plays a role in the outcome after stimuli is processed, we behave and that is it. All behaviour is perfect in the sense that it cannot be different, unless something else is also different. Awareness plays a role in our brain processes that produces the outcomes we manifest. The question is, what changes? I will discuss this in the final chapter that follows.

CHAPTER 8

WHAT NOW?

This book could end the centuries-old debate on free will simply by looking at it from a new perspective. This new approach is quite significant when we think about it and start recognizing it in our daily lives. Whether we believe we have free will or not, nothing changes, life goes on. We continue to feel as though we can do whatever we want, whenever we want. Even when we consider Procirclism as a valid approach to the development of behaviour, we still feel like that. There is nothing wrong with this feeling because that is how we are made. I believe the feeling serves a purpose. After I completed my procirclistic model, I realized that much changed while everything remained the same. What changed is an understanding of how choices are made, but we still feel we can do whatever we want. This is just a feeling, but it is enforced because we think we do what we want. I call this the *reality illusion*.

The key question is how do we arrive at what we want? There is a process we are not consciously aware of that produces our desires. Because we are not aware of these processes, and the fact that will comes to us milliseconds before we exhibit what we will, it feels that it is our choice. The following is an illustration of how this works. Imagine we must choose a number and just milliseconds before we choose a number, a large red number appears in front of us that only we can see. It is the number two hundred and fifty. Milliseconds later we choose a number and that number is two hundred and fifty. What we do not know is the process that took place outside our awareness that produced the number. When we chose two hundred and fifty, we chose it because we wanted it, and we wanted it because it was the result of a process that produced an outcome we manifested in choosing two hundred and fifty. Nevertheless, it feels as if we simply chose it for no reason. We feel we could have chosen any other number but wanted to choose two hundred and fifty. How it feels to us is not what happens, but because we are unaware of what happens (process) our feeling becomes reality to us.

Regarding the free will issue, we may wonder why philosophers have been preoccupied with it for centuries? Perhaps because our daily lives are continuously affected by the will of people. Great triumphs and horrible tragedies have occurred because of the will of people. The question on the tip of our tongue is why? Why has so much tragedy happened because of the will of people? Could they have chosen something different that would have avoided the tragedy? I would like to mention one of the world's most horrible tragedies that occurred because of the will of certain people: the Holocaust. It is not difficult to ask whether this tragedy could have been avoided. Many will say yes while others will say no. For this tragedy not to have occurred, something else would have had to be different. Some people may say that the Second World War and the Holocaust may never have happened if Hitler had not been born (or had not been rejected by the Academy of Fine Arts in Vienna). Perhaps you believe if the Treaty of Versailles (June 28, 1919), which ended the First World War had not been so hard on Germany, the conditions in Germany may not have been so bad that it would allow Hitler to take advantage and be elected Chancellor of Germany (January 30, 1933). Without going into further details, we can see that although the will of a certain group of people started the Second World War, we may also conclude that a multitude of factors (stimuli) contributed to the establishment of the will that started the war. We may even go so far as to say that if certain conditions had not existed at the time, the Second World War may never have happened. We all agree, I believe, that we are often greatly influenced by our environment and even more distant factors. Things that happened long ago may still affect our life today. Post-traumatic stress disorder is a well-known condition. If this idea is understood and accepted, Procirclism cannot be far behind. It is built on the same principle: that historical factors influence our choices as the brain processes them as stimuli. Procirclism keeps building on this principle and goes much deeper without changing a beat. If we agree that we are subject to influences and agree that we are not always aware of all the factors that influence us, then we understand that we relinquish some control over the consequences. If we agree that those influences—as part of the brain processes— play a role in our brain, then we may also conclude that unless we have control over the working of our brain, we have little control over the outcomes of the processes. Most of us have looked at the pros and cons before making a decision. At that time, we did not feel that we were not in control. We felt we could make any decision we wanted to. No argument here. But that does not mean it happens like that just because it feels that way to us.

For many years, society thought it should punish misbehaviour to correct it and many people followed a behaviour management path that was not effective. The undesired behaviour of children was met with punishment to create compliant and acceptable behaviour. However, punishment lacks understanding, insight, compassion, instruction, direction, skill building, respect and relationship building. It does not affect the processes that contribute to undesired behaviour in the first place. It is as if there is a scale and all the weights that contribute to undesired behaviour are being attacked with counterweights in the hope the scale tilts over to the desired behaviour. Instead of treating bad behaviour, the weight of punishment is placed on the scale and eventually it collapses. In this illustration, the scale will return to tipping over towards the undesired behaviour when the weights of punishment are removed or the effects of the punishment have worn out.

Procirclism is built on processes with the understanding that all stimuli being processed over our lifetime affect every outcome. I am not suggesting that we should never explain the logical consequences of undesired behaviour to a child, I merely suggest that punishment does not teach skills to cope with situations. It does not show compassion, acceptance or encouragement, nor does it validate the person. The most effective stimuli to create acceptable behaviour are left out. If punishment alone works and creates desirable behaviour, this world would be different today. Our prisons would not be so crowded, and far less people would break the law and commit repeat offences.

I have worked together with my wife for over twenty-five years with underprivileged children and have seen all kinds of behaviour, much of it aggressive and offensive, sometimes criminal. If punishment was effective, these young people would be model citizens because they did not lack punishment before coming into care.

Procirclism includes all stimuli. The source of the stimuli affects the outcome of brain processes. Compare this to the engine of a car. The motor is designed to run. When we start the engine, put the gears in drive and press the accelerator, we expect the car to drive and that is what usually happens. However, we must supply the fuel source and that must be gasoline or diesel. When we replace this with water, the engine will not drive no matter what we do. The fuel source is required in the process to make the engine run. As such, it affects the outcome.

In similar fashion, the brain processes stimuli. The kind of stimuli affect the kind of outcome, which means *what* we will. We can take this comparison one step further when we say water means the engine will not run while gasoline means it will.

I would like to provide one more comparison in behaviour management. Imagine you are driving a car that pulls heavily to the right. To keep the car driving straight, you pull with equal force to the left. When we release our grip, the car will drive off the road to the right. Unless the alignment of the car corrects itself miraculously, we need to see a mechanic to fix the alignment. We can look at behaviour management in the same way. Any forceful attempt to manage behaviour will not address the process (real issues). When we address the processes by treating different issues that affect behaviour as stimuli, we contribute to brain processes that include new stimuli. These affect outcomes so that the different outcomes are manifested in behaviour. We might say that it is a big improvement over previous behaviour. That is like the car that does not pull to the right after the alignment has been corrected. Looking more closely at the pros and cons, it becomes a little technical because no thought, whether pro or con, comes to mind because we wanted to think about it. The thoughts did not become known to us until they appeared on our awareness screen. We did not consciously pull them up from somewhere. If we did not pull them up but they came to us without our active involvement, then we must admit, if they affect our decision, it was not the result of our will.

When our decisions are based upon factors that are not chosen by us but come to us in the form they appear, then they influence the outcome—our decision. It is not a stretch of the imagination to recognize that, so far, there is no fragment left of a random, independent free will, that is void of any influence and makes the decision.

As you have read, Procirclism has departed from the free will issue and proclaims there is neither free will nor no free will. There is just will and that is the force necessary to manifest behaviour. What role does our feeling that we can do what we want play? It plays a major role because that is how we are designed. We would not feel that way if we were not meant to feel that way. Feeling that we have full control and can do as we please is a stimulus that is processed by the brain. It keeps us involved; together with the awareness factor it affects the processes of stimuli and the outcomes.

Although we are not robots, the feeling we can do as we please prevents us from believing we are robots. The belief that we have an independent free will that is void of any influential factors could be considered scary and unpredictable because anybody could do anything at any time. The belief that we do not have free will, however, tends to make humans kind of robotic. Procirclism does neither one. It does not give rise to fear, unpredictability or make us do anything, anytime, and it does not make humans robotic.

The essence of Procirclism is humanity in motion. It's complex and simple at the same time. The importance of our awareness factor and the complexity of the brain processes make it impossible to be like robots. There is a constant stream of stimuli being processed. Among that information are impulses and triggers that create thoughts. These thoughts may search for additional information and that information affects behaviour. Through our awareness factor, stimulated by triggers, we may seek sources that provide information which we know contributes to producing desired behaviour. What sources do we allow to influence us and why? The answer to why is embedded in this book and is the essence of Procirclism. What are the stimuli (information) that affect behaviour? What environment are we exposing our children to? Which books do we read or music we listen to and movies we watch? They all influence us whether we believe it or not. Yes, we may feel that we can do what we want but to what or whom do we give the power to design our will?

We experience several emotions throughout the day. These emotions happen to us. We don't will them upon us. It is not as if we tell ourselves that we want to feel happy now and it suddenly happens. Fear falls upon us and so does sadness or disappointment. However, emotions don't just happen. Feelings like sadness, enjoyment, happiness, disappointment or anger are all influenced by stimuli. We became angry because someone scratched our car or we felt happy because the estimate for our car repair was much lower than we anticipated.

We have little or no control over our feelings. Yet, through the awareness factor, our brain processes may produce informative thoughts, memories, etc. that produce certain feelings. We may choose to listen to music from the past and when we do, we experience happiness. Sometimes when we feel angry, we talk to someone and it helps us to settle down. When a misunderstanding upsets us, we may feel that way until a friend explains what really happened. We realize that we had perceived it all wrong and that it contributed to our anger. When we take this a step further, it is not difficult to imagine that people can provoke emotions in others by feeding them information to which they react in anger. Advertisements tend to do the same. They are skillfully designed to create a desire for a product often without the conscious awareness of the consumer. Emotions contribute to behaviour. Only when we are immune to any influential factors, and there are no reasons that contribute to our decisions and the question why we did something cannot be answered, can we then think about the existence of random, independent free will. This does not mean that the opposite must be true. Only when we ask the question of whether we have free will or not do we get into trouble. That question pushes us into a corner or rather a circle which has no beginning or end. It is a question to which there is no answer but when asked, we try desperately to answer it with yes or no. Procirclism escapes this trap. It does not answer whether we have free will or not. In fact, it does not recognize the question because it explains that will cannot be free nor not be free. In that sense, it supports all we do and want and the feeling that we can do whatever we want. In our minds, that is always what we do—exactly what we want.

Let us go back to how it feels to us. To us, it feels we can do what we want. Yet, when we change our mind we do not say that we changed it because we wanted to and that there is no other reason for it. On the contrary, we often give a reason why we changed our mind. If we are asked why we did it, we give a reason. This strongly suggests that a change of mind does not happen for no reason. It suggests that there are factors that influence us. However, we can only talk about the factors we know and feel, and that they weighed so heavily that they triggered a change of mind. What we do not know is the immense number of other influential factors the brain processes as stimuli over our lifetime that influenced our change of mind. The influential factor, which we recognized and used as the reason why we changed our mind, appeared as it did (was perceived) because of all the prior processes. That one factor we recognized as the reason why we changed our mind was perceived the way we did because our perception, which is dynamic and consistently in development, contributed to that. This happens at the unconscious level. My point is that we do not support an independent, random free will that is not subject to any influence. Our daily behaviour, as we can see so clearly in this example, demonstrates that nothing happens in a vacuum; there are reasons for what we do and do not do. That is what Procirclism explains.

Procirclism works for believers and unbelievers alike; it does not discriminate. If it did not apply to all people, I would not have written this book. Whether we believe in a supreme being or not, Procirclism accommodates all faiths. There is no need to adjust the belief we adhere to. In the procirclistic model, we influence each other in such a manner that the outcomes will be that people become more caring, understanding, accepting, sensitive and supportive. We raise our children in certain environments. We teach them and influence them daily. People affect each other in many ways. The information we receive through the media affects us. We are often unable to relate an experience to a behaviour we manifest because all the influences interrelate. They are included in the process of stimuli that produce outcomes we manifest in behaviour. What a fantastic world we could have, but reality shows different. Yet, it is perfect in the sense that it could not have been any different without different stimuli. The way we will be tomorrow depends on what has happened in our life up to this second.

I would like to go briefly over my own experience where one fragment which happened over thirty years ago is still affecting me today. I describe how it led from one thought to another until it reached a conclusion. When I started pondering the question of whether we have free will or not, it stimulated me to think about the reasons we have for the choices we make. My mind took me to a variety of influential factors such as emotions and perceptions. Next, I faced another hurdle. This hurdle put everything seamlessly together after I had figured it out. Will became the center of my attention. To determine whether it is free or not, it needed to be defined. What is will?

I remember exactly where I was when the definition of will came to my mind. I was on a long-distance run when it happened. I had my cell phone with me and took a picture of the spot where I was when the thought came to me: *Will is the force necessary to manifest behaviour.* That definition produced another thought: *Will is neither free nor not free.*

For me, it was the glue that put it all together. I was surprised because this option had never crossed my mind. I had been occupied with the question of whether we have or do not have free will and it surprised me when suddenly the thought appeared in my mind that will is neither free nor not free. When defining will as the force necessary to manifest behaviour, it completes Procirclism and makes it a seamless concept.

Our brain is so important that our life depends on it. Brain structure and its functionality is different in each person. Our brain is the central command post.

It makes no difference whether we believe or do not believe we have free will. Our belief does not change any facts. When we discuss the topic, we use arguments to support one position or the other. I believe that too often a predisposition affects the way we use supporting arguments for our position. At the same time, we may overlook weaknesses of any arguments we bring forward in support of our predisposition, but ignore arguments that support the opposing position as we try to weaken them. When we ponder over questions, our brain will find its way to wherever it may lead as it examines thoughts that appear and relate to the issue. As a result, we may arrive at a completely different and possibly surprising position. Frequently with philosophical topics we may taint the outcome when trying to prove a position we hold. The process is usually the most important element of any development, rather than the outcome. If I need to learn from it, I would learn more from the process that causes us to arrive at one position or another than from the outcome itself. I believe that all behaviour is predictable but cannot be predicted. The intriguing element of knowledge is that more knowledge makes us realize there is more we don't know. Knowledge, the unknown and the realization that we don't know, are stimuli that are processed by the brain and affect the outcome. If today is not a good day, tomorrow will be better (or worse) because of what we did yesterday. When doing what we feel we want, we wonder how that want is established. We may look at things differently when arguing with one another; when feeling angry at another person; when assuming something that triggers an emotion and affects our perception that causes misunderstandings that reduce our enjoyment or happiness at the time. We may look at the behaviour of our children differently and wonder what their sources of information (stimuli) are that affect their behaviour. We may wonder what needs to be done if behaviour could not have been different unless something was different. Perhaps it makes us wonder whether we could have made that difference. That is a powerful revolutionary thought that influences the behaviour of tomorrow and beyond.

Thinking about free will is a tremendous experience and enjoyment for me. I did not start by trying to defend any pre-assumed position on the free will issue; I just started thinking and it produced an outcome that surprised me. I routinely apply the procirclistic model to observations. It works every time. I have become more aware of what I allow myself to be influenced by and I am more aware of my emotions and beliefs and how they affect my behaviour. I still feel as if I can do what I want and when I want it, I just frequently ask what made me want it, or feel a certain way or believe something. I agree, we do what we want and that is the essence of our humanity, and a powerful stimulus in Procirclism. What we do, we do because it is the only thing we can do at the time we do it. That is because what we do is the result of process rather than choice. Yet it is true as Einstein once said: "Every man can do what he wants but he cannot will what he wants."

Free will, do you have it? I have provided you with a new approach that applies to all of us, you and me included. For me, it ends the debate at least, and I use the procirclistic approach regularly. I apply it to myself when analyzing my choices. I try to create repetitive reminders to increase my awareness of all stimuli that my brain receives and where I possibly can to become aware of them. Using this new approach, I now often see other people in a different light, with a better understanding, which in turn affects my behaviour towards others. When I say that I now often understand other people better, I mean that I understand there are numerous factors that play a role in a process that determines an outcome and as such, behaviour, even when I do not know all those factors or how the complex process exactly works that produces outcomes, thus behaviour.

Following the statements of these two great men, I conclude by saying that among the greatest dangers we face, is the silent force of destructive manipulation, at least that is how I see it. Many of us are unaware, fail to believe, or simply do not recognize it. This makes it an even greater danger and puts a powerful, destructive weapon in the hands of those who skillfully use it to manipulate others for a variety of self-serving and often harmful reasons. The evidence of this powerful phenomenon is all around us and clearly visible for those who can see. I realize I may not be able to make you believe me, but neither can I change the truth. I hope this book enhances our awareness and opens eyes, causing us to see from a new perspective. Happiness, peace, contentment and compassion are all the result of a process rather than choice—most likely a complex process, but nevertheless a process. Subsequently, we should often ask ourselves the following question. What is the source, internal or external, of the information that influences the processes in our brain, that affect, if not determine, our behaviour?

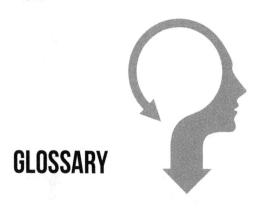

GLOSSARY

I have added this brief glossary to define the meaning of some of the words I have used to enhance the understanding of this book. The meaning of those words, as defined in this glossary, apply only to the content of the book.

Awareness factor – When we become consciously aware (being aware that we are aware) of something, it becomes a stimulus that is being processed by the brain with other stimuli. As such it factors in (contributes to) the outcome of the process of all stimuli and referred to as the awareness factor.

Awareness platform – Used to illustrate that the ability, of that which handles our awareness, is a significant factor regarding the moments we can become aware of in respect of its time. For instance, is the moment one second, a tenth, a hundredth of a second, or a smaller moment we can become aware of.

Awareness screen – It is an illustrative description of our awareness. We can picture that something is pushed to that screen before we can see it as is the case with everything that shows on a computer screen. We cannot see anything on the computer screen before it is displayed on it. It is used to demonstrate when we become consciously aware of something. When something appears on our awareness screen it means we become consciously aware of it.

Brain process – The brain seamlessly continually processes all information/influences as stimuli.

I – Answers the question *who* does the thinking, choosing* etc. When not in italic it is primarily used for identifying purposes, meaning I, and nobody else but me.

I – Answers the question: what does the thinking? However, *I* needed to be clearly defined as it is done in this book. After that, the I's can be merged and expressed as *I*. Depending on what is said, it can mean who, what or both. I had to make the distinction between I and *I* to lead up to this point. Without it, this book could not have been written.

Influential factor – Any influence that factors in (affects or contributes to) an outcome or choice. When something is free of an influential factor it means nothing has influenced or affected the outcome or choice.

Interpretation factor – Used to demonstrate that it matters and has an impact how we interpret something. Depending how we interpret something it has a greater or lesser influence on an outcome.

Manifested behaviour – When we behave in any way it is related to as manifestation (showing, demonstrating) of behaviour. He behaved angrily, he manifested angry behaviour.

Outcomes – The results of a process. In this case the results of the process of stimuli in the brain.

Perception – How we perceive, interpret something. This can greatly vary between individuals.

Perception factor – Used to indicate that perception, how we see things or perceive them to be, factors in (influences) the process and thus in the outcome.

Procirclism – This is the concept answering the question why, and the content of this book. The word is made up as follows: *Pro* comes from the word process (the brain processes all information/influences as stimuli). *Circ* comes from the word circle (the outcome of the processing of stimuli affect the next process of stimuli and repeats itself after each process). *Ism* is added to make it a noun.

Reality illusion – Something feels real but is in fact an illusion perceived as real and unknown to us that it is an illusion. We are not aware it is an illusion.

Stimulus/stimuli – Anything that affects the brain and is processed by the brain is called a stimulus. From information to experiences and observations. A stimulus can have an internal and external source. Food, including medications odours, colours and temperatures, to mention some are all stimuli.

Threshold – a minimum requirement for something to take place. For instance, for water to turn into ice it requires that the temperature should be below zero Celsius. So, zero Celsius is the threshold. In the book I mention threshold, as something that is required before something else can take place. I did not describe the specifics of that threshold, because it may not be known, or it may be known but when more discoveries are made, that threshold may change. I use the term to demonstrate that something takes place but there is a minimum requirement for it to take place, whatever that requirement may be.

Weighing factor – Something weighs more or less. In other words, it has more or less of an impact on the outcome. The weighing factor is used to indicate that something factors (affects) in the outcome and it may have more or less of an influence on the outcome. Today there will be a soccer match, but it is raining heavily. The soccer match will be indoors. Because it will be held indoors the rain has very little, if any, influence on the game and therefore has an insignificant weighing factor.

*Example. I choose to buy this book. We can ask who chooses, and we can ask what chooses. Each question has a distinctly different answer.

ABOUT
THE AUTHOR

 I would like to take this opportunity to briefly introduce myself. I was an immigrant to Canada but have since become a Canadian. I am a husband, father, father-in-law, grandfather, brother, brother-in-law, uncle and to some a friend. Faith is a continuous process helping me to be a better person. I have always been curious and the question *why?* is often at the tip of my tongue. I believe it may even be the most asked question. I have never found a simple answer as to why my favourite sport is soccer followed by cycling, and for the last thirty-plus years, jogging. I still ask myself, after a difficult long-distance run: Why? I guess there is no arguing with a healthy addiction.

From early on I was always interested in psychology, philosophy, history, and much later, some politics. I also enjoy the simple exercise of thinking. I like a good debate and a progressive exchange of thoughts as well as the exploration of new concepts and ideas; it can be fascinating. For more than twenty-five years my wife and I have been working with underprivileged children and youth. Currently we run our own organization and are serving the needs of the children and youth in our care. The need to think is always present. It may not come as a surprise that behaviour is very often on our mind. More than thirty years ago, I was asked a question that I have pondered for many years. Ultimately, after many years, it resulted in the creation of this book. Its content is in many ways applicable to the work we do, however, not only to our work but to all aspects of our life as we always manifest behaviour. I guess I could argue that behaviour is the result of process rather than choice.

CPSIA information can be obtained
at www.ICGtesting.com
Printed in the USA
LVHW021107060721
691954LV00003B/431